Hospital End User Computing in Japan How to Use FileMaker Pro with Hospital Information Systems

Editor

Shunji Wakamiya

Department of Ophthalmology
Kawasaki Medical School
Japan

Co-Editors

Kazunobu Yamauchi

Faculty of Medical Information & Management Science
School of Health Sciences, Fujita Health University
Japan

&

Hiroyuki Yoshihara

Department of Medical Informatics
Graduate School of Medicine Kyoto University
Japan

CONTENTS

FOREWORD

The system of Medical information has seen progress. It began with the streamlining of medical accounting, promoting order entries, and then computerizing medical records. All of those innovations have been contributing not only to reducing the wait time but also to improving medical safety, making an end of handwritten requests, preventing patient mix-ups, *etc.* Now that the contents of medical records are to be also integrated into medical information system, what is going to be required? It is absolutely necessary to support medical care for patients through the promotion of the information sharing of team medicine. The promotion of education and research, early detection of side-effects, and the creation of clinical evidence, as well as guidelines, will be also required.

In order to satisfy those requirements, vast amounts of data of Organized Computing - a hospital information system which contributes to medical management - is essential, End User Computing – a tool that can easily exteriorize users' effective ideas – is suitable for the application and analysis of the data. When we combine these two factors, we are confronted with the following three issues:

- The Hospital information system has yet to standardize its data output format,
- To realize a secure connection between the former that aims to be isolated from the Internet and the latter that requires the use of the Internet,
- How to generate documentation for the latter in the case where it is incorporated into medical treatment.

With regard to the first issue, as the Ministry of Health, Labor, and Welfare set eight standards in March, 2010, it is expected that each medical information system will be equipped with standard information output function. In terms of the second and the third issues, the previous similar books have gone no further than noting their convenience and flexibility, and this is the first book that has successfully referred to those issues.

I sincerely hope that this book will help the readers contribute to further promoting medical science and medical care in research and educational processes, and that this will also help improve the readers' medical operating environment such as preparation of documents and reports.

Michio Kimura, MD, PhD

Medical Information Department
Hamamatsu University, School of Medicine
Japan Association for Medical Informatics (JAMI), Director General
Japan

PREFACE

This book is intended for readers who wish to efficiently improve the environment of medical treatment and care, such as staff engaged in medical clinics or hospitals, and vendors targeting medical information systems. Medical information systems are generally introduced to medical facilities by vendors who fulfill the functional criteria of medical information systems when each facility develops and introduces these systems. However, many medical staffs with experience of using medical information systems may feel that such systems developed by vendors do not always provide a good working environment for medical staff. Therefore, medical facilities cannot always make the huge investments necessary to construct medical information systems implementing all of the functions requested by medical staff. This book discusses ways of addressing these issues. Although, there have been many reports regarding computerization within hospital departments or personal work, there have been a few reports in the English literature concerning end user computing as a method of computerization implemented in the whole hospital. End user computing has been widely adopted in the field of medical treatment and care in Japan, but it has not been adopted around the world as there have been few reports in English. The main purpose of this book is to share our experiences regarding end user applications with workers outside Japan. Medical information systems have developed from receipt processing systems to electronic medical records through order entry systems since the 1970s, and are now shifting toward electronic health records. These systems have been introduced at various facilities by organizational computing. In contrast to the flow of such organizational computing, many applications supporting medical workflow by end user computing have recently been reported in Japan. FileMaker Pro is a common tool in end user computing, especially in Japan, and can be used in the whole hospital, between or among departments, for individual departments, and for individuals within an organization. Some end user application systems cooperate with hospital information systems, and some such systems have been developed and introduced by end users. Therefore, we selected end user application systems in Japan and focused in this book on how to use FileMaker Pro with hospital information systems. This book will provide new viewpoints regarding future hospital information systems and will offer advice to achieve cooperation between end user applications and hospital information systems, how end user applications are implemented, and the most important points in the development of medical information systems that give priority to the effectiveness of medical workflows or collection of medical data.

Shunji Wakamiya

Department of Ophthalmology
Kawasaki Medical School
Japan

Kazunobu Yamauchi

Faculty of Medical Information & Management Science
School of Health Sciences, Fujita Health University
Japan

&

Hiroyuki Yoshihara

Department of Medical Informatics
Graduate School of Medicine Kyoto University
Japan

List of Contributors

Akira Ohtahara

Division of Cardiology, San-in Rosai Hospital
1-8-1 Kaike-Shinden, Yonago, Tottori, Japan
ohtahara@saninh.rofuku.go.jp

Atsuhiko Okagaki

Department of Gynecology, Osaka National Hospital
2-1-14 Hoenzaka, Chuo-Ku, Osaka, Japan
okagaki3@onh.go.jp

Hiroshi Hara

Department of Internal Medicine, Haradoi Hospital
6-40-8 Aoba, Higashi-Ku, Fukuoka, Japan
hisyo@haradoi-hospital.com

Hiroyuki Yoshihara

Department of Medical Informatics
Graduate School of Medicine Kyoto University
Yoshida-Konoe, Sakyo-Ku, Kyoto, Japan
lob@kuhp.kyoto-u.ac.jp

Kazunobu Yamauchi

Faculty of Medical Information & Management Science,
School of Health Sciences, Fujita Health University
1-98 Dengakugakubo, Kutsukake, Toyoake, Aichi, Japan
kyamauti@fujita-hu.ac.jp

Kazutoshi Matsunami

Department of Gynecology, Matsunami General Hospital
185-1 Tashiro, Kasamatsu, Hashima-Gun, Gifu, Japan
mgh2@matsunami-hsp.or.jp

Osamu Sato

Department of Business Administration, Tokyo Keizai University
1-7-34 Minami-Machi, Kokubunji, Tokyo, Japan
osamsato@tku.ac.jp

Shinsuke Hiramatsu

Department of Obstetrics and Gynecology, Nippon Steel Hirohata Hospital
3-1 Yumesaki, Hirohata-Ku, Himeji, Hyogo, Japan
s_hiramatsu@hirohata-hp.or.jp

Shigeru Yoshida

Medical IT Center, Nagoya University Hospital
65 Tsurumai, Showa-Ku, Nagoya, Aichi, Japan
shigeru@med.nagoya-u.ac.jp

Shunji Wakamiya

Department of Ophthalmology, Kawasaki Medical School
577 Matsushima, Kurashiki, Okamaya, Japan
oph@mtj.biglobe.ne.jp

Shunsuke Hotokezaka

Department of Orthopedics, Saga Prefectural Hospital Koseikan
1-12-9 Mizugae, Saga, Japan
hotokezs@ortho.med.kyushu-u.ac.jp

Tatsuhiko Koga

Department of Internal Medicine, Haradoi Hospital
6-40-8 Aoba, Higashi-Ku, Fukuoka, Japan
tatskoga@qf6.so-net.ne.jp

Tetsu Nakamura

Department of Radiology, Kakogawa East City Hopital
797-295 Isshiki, Hiraoka, Kakogawa, Hyogo, Japan
t-nakamura@kakohp.jp

Tsukasa Tsunoda

Director, Kawasaki Medical School Hospital
577 Matsushima, Kurashiki, Okamaya, Japan
ttsukasa@med.kawasaki-m.ac.jp

Yasuhito Yamamoto

Department of Pediatrics, Tokyo Metropolitan Hiroo General Hospital
2-34-10 Ebisu, Shibuya-Ku, Tokyo, Japan
yamamoto@medicalmac.com

Yosimune Shiratori

Medical Information Department, Gifu University Hospital
1-1 Yanagido, Gifu, Japan
tara@gifu-u.ac.jp

CHAPTER 1

Definition and Classification of End User Computing in This Book

Shunji Wakamiya[1,*], Kazunobu Yamauchi[2], Hiroyuki Yoshihara[3], Tsukasa Tsunoda[4] and Osamu Sato[5]

[1]Kawasaki Medical School; [2]Fujita Health University; [3]Graduate School of Medicine Kyoto University; [4]Kawasaki Medical School Hospital and [5]Tokyo Keizai University, Japan

Abstract: In this book, we define "organizational computing" as computing where vendors assume responsibility for the development of systems or software, and "end user computing" as computing where the responsibility is assumed by the end users themselves. Moreover, we define "institutional computing (I-type)" and "staff computing (S-type)" as computing environments where systems or software is developed by staff within and outside the division of information and systems, respectively. We classify end user applications into three categories: systems in which electronic information moves interactively between hospital information systems and end user applications, systems in which electronic information moves in one direction only from the former systems to the latter applications, and systems that have no cooperation between the two.

Keywords: Definition, institutional computing, staff computing, organizational computing, classification, I-type, S-type, end user applications, information systems, environments.

1. DEFINITION OF END USER COMPUTING IN THIS BOOK

The advantages and disadvantages of end user computing in the field of medical treatment and care are the same as in other fields. However, there are differences in the implementation of end user computing between medical fields and, for example, the needs of industry. This is because medical facilities are composed of various medical professions and they cannot be easily reshuffled, although no qualification is usually needed in industry or enterprise environments. Moreover, training for end user computing is controlled by the division of information and systems in ordinary enterprise environments, although it is controlled by end

***Address correspondence to Shunji Wakamiya:** Department of Ophthalmology, Kawasaki Medical School, Japan; E-mail: oph@mtj.biglobe.ne.jp

users, especially medical doctors themselves, who have a great deal of authority in medical treatment and care environments. Here, it should be noted that the term "end user computing" may be used differently in each field. Brancheau and Brown defined end user computing in 1993 as "the adoption and use of information technology by personnel outside the information systems department to DEVELOP software applications in support of organizational tasks" [1]. However, it is difficult to apply this definition to the field of medical treatment and care because most of the division of information and systems in hospitals function as end users to vendors, except at some limited university hospitals or medical school hospitals. Most general hospitals are comparable to small businesses and small-scale enterprises. Therefore, it is necessary to have the proper definition of end user computing in the field of medical treatment and care, although it does not alter the fact that end user computing conflicts with organizational computing. Here, we define "organizational computing" as computing where vendors assume responsibility for the development of systems or software, and "end user computing" as computing where this responsibility is assumed by the end users themselves. Moreover, we define "institutional computing (I-type)" and "staff computing (S-type)" as computing environments where systems or software is developed by staff within and outside the division of information and systems, respectively. We will introduce a number of cases of end user computing according to these concepts. This definition was advocated in a symposium about end user computing held at the 29th Joint Conference on Medical Informatics in Hiroshima in 2009 [2].

2. CLASSIFICATION OF END USER APPLICATION IN THIS BOOK

End user applications in this book are classified according to the method of connection with hospital information systems, as organizational computing plays a large role and hospital information systems are representative of organizational computing. Therefore, we classify end user applications into three categories: systems in which electronic information moves interactively between hospital information systems and end user applications, systems in which electronic information moves in one direction only from the former systems to the latter applications, and systems that have no cooperation between the two. Methods by which cooperation is achieved between the former systems and the latter applications differ between hospitals. Please read the corresponding papers in chapters II to IV.

CONFLICT OF INTEREST

None declared.

ACKNOWLEDGEMENT

None declared.

REFERENCES

[1] Brancheau JC, Brown CV. The Management of end-user computing: Status and directions. ACM Computing Surveys 1993; 25(4): 437-82.

[2] Tsunoda T, Wakamiya S, Sato O, Yamauchi K. Merits and demerits of EUC from the viewpoint of hospital management. Japan Journal of Medical Informatics 2009; 29(Suppl): 151-55.

CHAPTER 2

Construction of a Clinical Decision Support System

Yasuhito Yamamoto*

Tokyo Metropolitan Hiroo General Hospital, Japan

Abstract: Computerized decision support system (CDSS) has demonstrated its efficacy in improving clinical practices and patient outcomes. HiPER 2.0 (Hiroo Information System for Pediatrics and ER, version 2.0), which the current authors have developed, is a system with an arrangement and techniques of processing and disseminating information different from those mentioned earlier in CDSS. HiPER 2.0 can collect a large amount of complex medical information. For example, order entry information at the time of empirical treatment was prescribed and its dosage was provided to the ICT and intervened to improve the effectiveness of nosocomial infection control. The system was not designed merely to perform intelligent processing with machines, rather, the CDSS was designed to encourage team care and facilitate rather than diminish opportunities for medical personnel to consult with specialists. New interfaces with enhanced "awareness" may alter views on CDSS and allow humans to better coexist with them.

Keywords: Medical safety, CDSS (Clinical decision support systems), DWH (Data warehouse), syndromic surveillance, OLAP, data cube, therapeutic drug monitoring, infection control, H1N1 influenza pandemic, real-time decision-making.

1. INTRODUCTION

Computerized decision support system (CDSS) is believed to have the potential to improve the quality of health care delivery. CDSSes are defined as information systems designed to improve clinical decision-making. They have demonstrated their efficacy in improving clinical practices and patient outcomes [1-5]. CDSSes have a long history stretching back as far as the 1970s and AAP Help. AAP Help had better accuracy at diagnosing acute abdominal pain than clinicians, it reduced mortality rates and unnecessary surgery, and it cut cases of perforation of the appendix in half. Systems such as reminder systems and consultation systems that

***Address correspondence to Yasuhito Yamamoto:** Department of Pediatrics, Tokyo Metropolitan Hiroo General Hospital, Japan; E-mail: yamamoto@medicalmac.com

Shunji Wakamiya, Kazunobu Yamauchi and Hiroyuki Yoshihara (Eds)

were not limited to providing clinical decision support were developed and proved successful [5].

The current healthcare environment, with its focus on improved quality of care, requires that the question no longer be, do we need a CDSS? but rather, How can we achieve a CDSS?

What has been gleaned from successful examples of CDSSes is that the S/N ratio is crucial. A warning system that is too sensitive and that generates a substantial amount of noise may unfortunately be ignored. Conversely, a system that is too cautious may sound warnings that come too little, too late. HiPER 2.0 which the current authors have developed is a system with an arrangement and techniques of processing and disseminating information different from those mentioned earlier.

2. METHODS

We firstly developed CDSS linked EMR that can collect a large amount of complex medical information. Order entry information at the time empirical treatment is prescribed and their dosage was provided to the ICT and intervened to improve the effectiveness of nosocomial infection control.

2.1. Comparison of HiPER 2.0 to Conventional CDSSes Using DWHs

The main system of a CDSS has a massive amount of medical information, and processing this information in real time is difficult without affecting the main system. HiPER 2.0, a unique platform to facilitate rapid development and provide high-speed processing, was constructed at this hospital to indicate information to relevant parties when appropriate. Bidirectional coordination of information with the main system emphasizes collecting all information in real time without distinguishing the type of information. HiPER 2.0 encompasses the information on the main system, which includes basic information, orders, information on carrying out those orders, notes, lab test results, and information on patient physical status. This information can vary in size from 170 to 3,000 fields, which include tracking of changes and where the information was created. This can lead to 8 million transactions a year, and processing servers run in parallel to ensure real-time performance even at peak times (Table **1**).

Table 1: Transactions that occur in one year

Type of Data	Transactions
Outpatient order	750,000
Outpatient execution	350,000
Inpatient order	2,060,000
Inpatient execution	2,650,000
Progress note	630,000
Nurse's note	1,060,000
Diagnostic code	350,000
Lab text results	480,000
Outpatient check-in info.	230,000
Patient status info.	200,000

To reduce communication and locking between servers, tables were horizontally partitioned in light of capacity and relevance, *e.g.*, information on carrying out of orders is partitioned into orders for wards and orders for outpatients and notes are partitioned into those from physicians and those from nurses. Related data such as the medication prescribed, prescription code, and dose that were included in a transaction were not vertically partitioned. Related data were joined and stored in a variable-length string field with the same structure and without creating indexes. Fig. (**1**), to achieve distributed processing, partitioning and joining were performed simultaneously, unlike in conventional DWHs.

2.2. The CAP Theorem and EDOL

Entering information in electronic medical records is not as important as providing medical care, so in clinical settings digital information may include extras and omissions and thus not necessarily reflect current conditions. HiPER 2.0 was designed to perform intelligent processing the instant when eventual consistency between current conditions and digital information is achieved and to immediately make those results available for use.

According to the CAP theorem [6], data consistency, system availability, and partition-tolerance (distribution) cannot be achieved simultaneously in the processes of parallel processing. By taking eventual consistency into account,

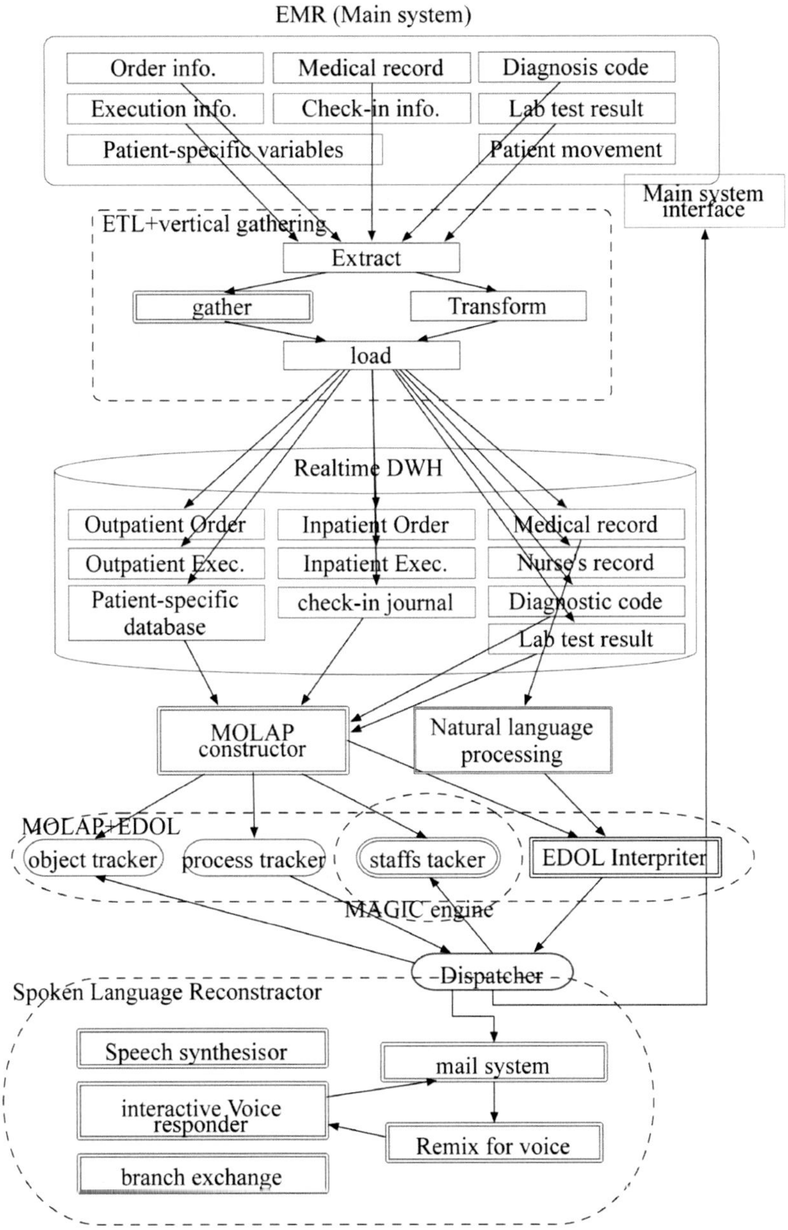

Figure 1: System diagram.

HiPER 2.0 can more readily provide parallel processing. The said, intelligent processing parameters, processing status, and interim results are kept distributed to perform intelligent processing in parallel. Thus, EDOL was developed to express the status of intelligent processing, including interim results. In terms of intelligent processing of medical information, the already standardized Arden Syntax is preferable in light of its definitions, mixing with other languages, and distribution, but Arden Syntax was not created to allow the display of interim results. EDOL is predicated on medical knowledge and was used in part of the current system's intelligent processing.

2.3. Infection Control Team (ICT) Intervention

Order entry information at the time of empirical treatment is prescribed and its dosage was provided to the ICT and intervened to improve the effectiveness of nosocomial infection control.

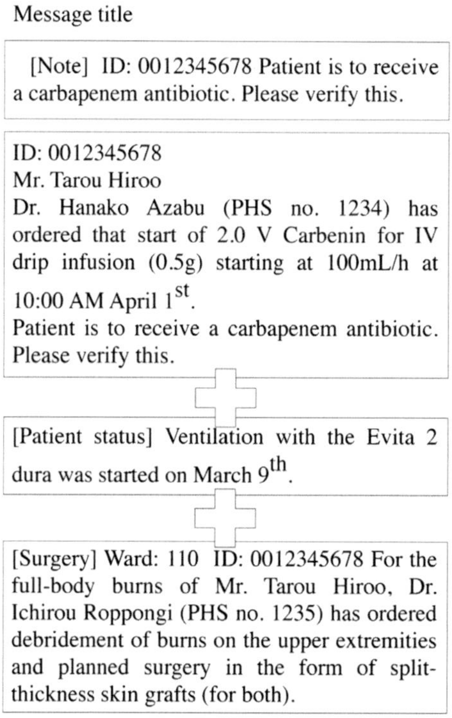

Figure 2: A sample of electronically available documents in ICT support systems.

Fig. (**2**), to allow the ICT to quickly ascertain the patient's status prior to administering drugs, the patient's overall status was ascertained and sent to the ICT. To improve efficiency of prescription confirmation, in December 2007 a CDSS supported immediate order processing. The number of days for prescription confirmation before and after supporting the system was compared.

2.4. A Framework for Chemotherapy Safety

A framework was constructed to allow chemotherapy to be administered smoothly and safely. Once they have formulated the chemotherapy protocol into orders, physicians decide whether or not to administer chemotherapy in light of the patient's status just prior to treatment. Based on the physician's decision, a specialized pharmacist prepares the medication.

Fig. (**3**), the physician has to confirm whether or not chemotherapy will be administered beforehand, but the EMR lacked the ability to list patients to receive chemotherapy, which made the work more complicated. HiPER 2.0 sends a chemotherapy list to the physician a day before and prompts entry of the physician's decision.

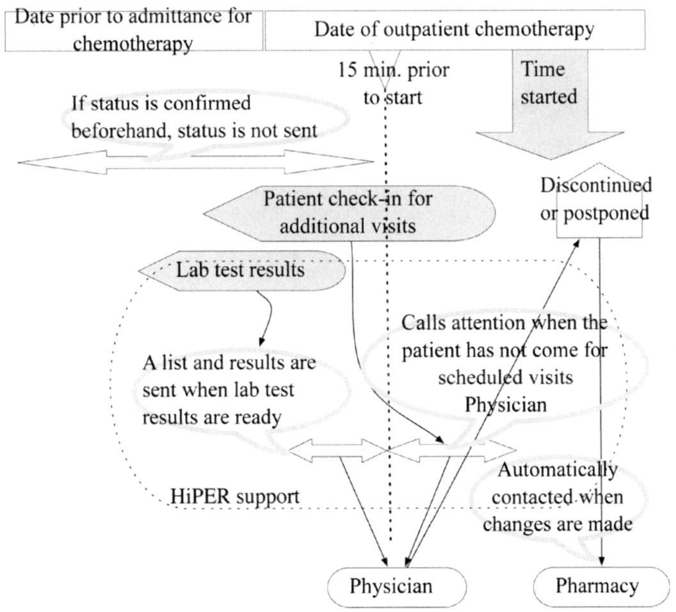

Figure 3: A framework for chemotherapy smoothly and safely.

2.5. An Automatic Syndromic Surveillance System

Syndromic surveillance is concerned with continuous monitoring of public health-related information sources and early detection of adverse disease events. The origins of the recent increase in the use of syndromic surveillance can be traced to the United States. One of the first syndromic surveillance systems to evolve from the anti-terrorist response was started in New York City, where ED patient attendances with 'chief complaints' are monitored on a daily basis [7].

In the recent years, a number of syndromic surveillance approaches have been proposed [8]. About 100 sites throughout the country have implemented and deployed syndromic surveillance systems with the Centers for Disease Control and Prevention (CDC) [9]. The goal of these systems is to enable earlier detection of epidemics and a more timely public health response, hours or days before disease clusters are recognized clinically, or before specific diagnoses are made and reported to public health authorities.

We developed an automatic syndromic surveillance system with the purpose of early detection of the outbreak of infectious diseases that can present epidemiologic information to the ICT.

Then, natural language processing was needed to identify important information in physician reports. Because, the entry interface is part of the main system client, so most of the information entered is standardized, but physician reports have not been adequately standardized.

Physician reports are specialized documents, so a new natural language processing engine was created to improve accuracy. A dictionary for semantic analysis was created by selecting a corpus of 200,000 physician reports from 1.35 million physician reports. Information selected from physician reports using natural language processing was used in syndromic surveillance, like that to detect outbreaks of new strains of influenza, and to convert physician reports to EDOL (*via* an interpreter). To measure the accuracy of natural language processing, 650,000 different physician reports were selected. With an error of 2%, a confidence level of 5%, and a population proportion of 10% and a sample size of 865 reports, random numbers of 83,654 reports were selected (including the representative corpus) and accuracy was measured.

2.6. Control of Communications and Prediction of Behavior

Information is disseminated not only onscreen on EMR but also by phone using audible tones, Short Message Service, and high-quality speech synthesis. HiPER

2.0 is connected with the main system but does not necessarily display information *via* the main system; it disseminates information *via* voice and button-activated messages accessed by PHS. PHS is originally a digital cordless telephone with the capability to handover from one cell to another. PHS cells are small, with transmission power of base station a maximum of 80 mW and range typically measures in tens of meters. Consequently, this improved the timing when information was conveyed and allowed greater access from different sites, allowing information to be disseminated the instant eventual consistency is achieved. If, for example, the party receiving information is busy with another call or is disconnected, the individual can switch to a brief message that remains in the logs. In addition, the party disseminating information needs not to be limited to a single party, meaning that information can be forwarded and distributed. For instance, with regard to prescriptions for outpatients, an anticoagulant dosage-monitoring assistant was used to detect irregularities. If noted, a pharmacist was asked about them. Fig. (**4**), if necessary, the pharmacist was able to contact the prescribing physician with a single click.

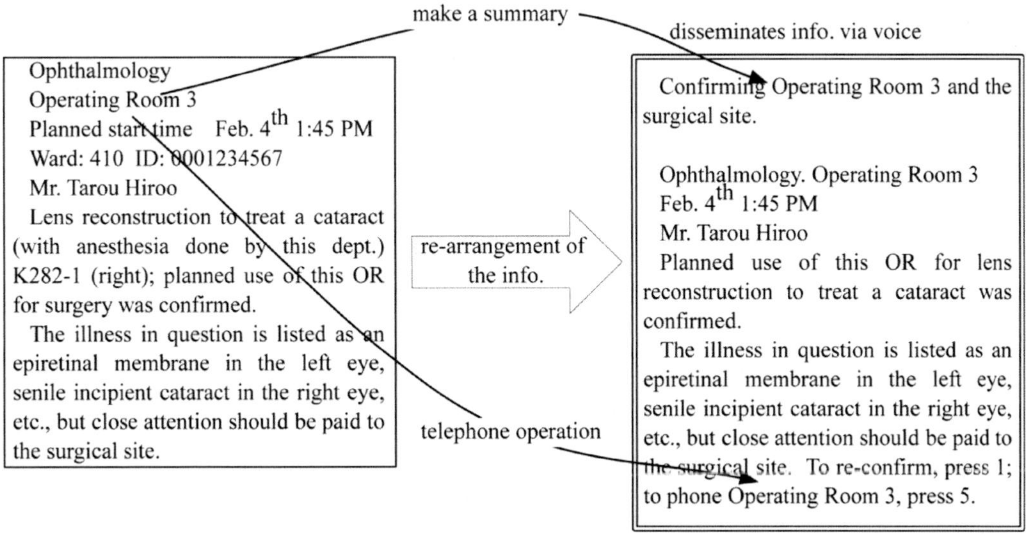

Figure 4: Re-arranging information for the clinician to discern linearly.

The system was not designed merely to perform intelligent processing with machines; rather, the CDSS was designed to encourage team care and facilitate rather than diminish opportunities for medical personnel to consult with specialists. Intelligent processing is not based on information prior to entry into the main system; rather, it is based on subsequent corrections and additional information from other parties, providing "control of communications" to warn a number of medical personnel or facilitate consultations with specialists. To achieve this, the system had to ascertain what the recipient was doing at that moment.

The location of medical personnel was automatically determined based on information on outpatient status, surgery, scheduled tests, and related information on patient movements. Analysis of the work done by physicians, subsequent identification of their patterns of behavior, and information on the location of their PHS were combined to calculate whether or not the physician would be able to answer his phone with a high level of accuracy.

3. RESULTS

3.1. ICT Intervention

Over a period of 6 months, information was provided to the ICT in 459 instances (average of 2.5 a day), and the ICT intervened in 48 instances. This figure accounted for 53% of all of the requests for the ICT to intervene. Prior to system implementation, therapeutic drug monitoring (TDM) was done on an average of 0.42, and this improved to 8.43 times ($p<0.05$) after that. The time before checking prescriptions by an infection control pharmacist decreased from 1.90 days to 1.19 days ($p<0.05$).

3.2. A Framework for Chemotherapy Safety

When compared the time immediately after the system implemented with 6 months later, the accuracy of confirmation improved from 45% to 65%.

3.3. An Automatic Syndromic Surveillance System

Results indicated that target phrases were identified from natural sentences with an accuracy of 95.3%. This natural language processing had the ability to correctly exclude phrases with differing subjects and phrases indicating potentiality, *e.g.,* "my older brother has a fever" and "I was told to come back if I developed a fever". The current system was used in syndromic surveillance to monitor outbreaks of new strains of influenza. The number of outbreaks by syndrome in the past 24 hours was tallied 5,000 times and compared with the results of multivariate analysis; outbreaks of new strains of influenza were detected without using a rapid diagnostic test for influenza or information on the illness. (Fig. **5**) Alerts were generated 62 times and they detected 56 of 135 days of outbreaks of the H1N1 influenza pandemic that occurred in summer 2009. Sensitivity, specificity and positive predictive value were 41.5%, 96.7% and 90.3%, respectively. (Fig. **6**).

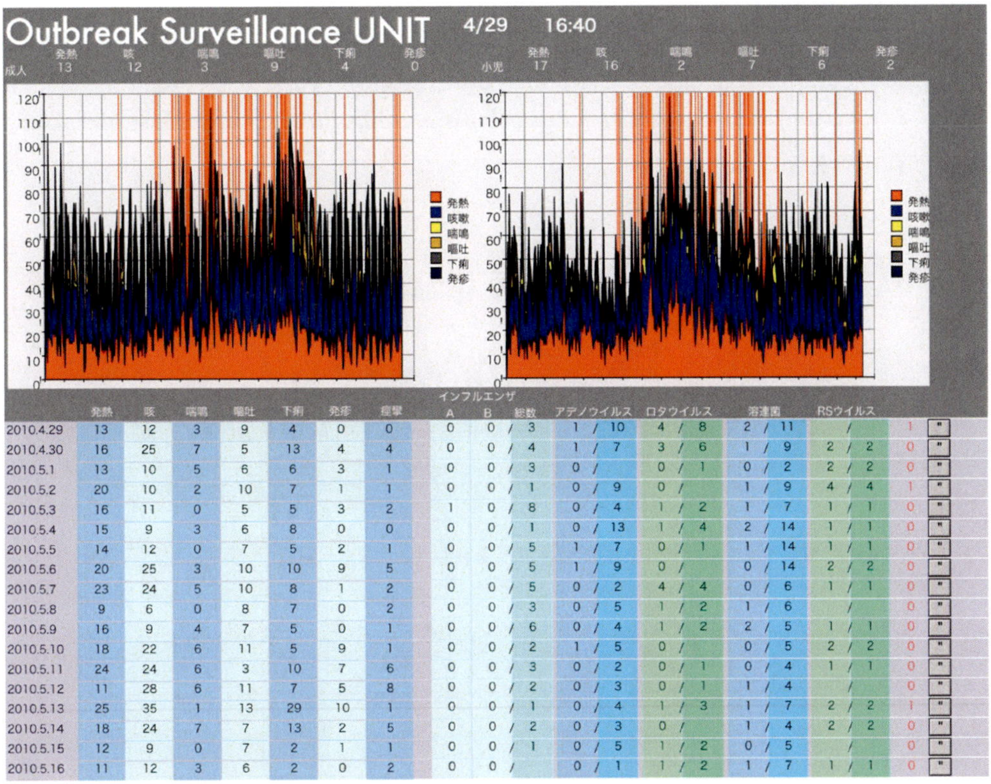

Figure 5: An automatic syndromic surveillance system.

3.4. Control of Communications and Prediction of Behavior

The location of medical personnel was automatically determined based on the location of the client used and the individual's work. The task was to improve the accuracy of determining an individual's location during his or her intermittent use of the client. Here, the intermittent use of appointment information and information on patient movements allowed the physician's focus to be predicted to an extent. Moreover, predicted information and information on the location of the individual's PHS were compared and prediction accuracy was measured. Results indicated that the location of 83% of physicians overall could be determined automatically for 30% or more of working hours (2 hrs 40 min). Highly intensive work such as performing surgery and seeing outpatients was misidentified as less intensive work at a rate of 4% ± 6, and there was less error with this than with the location of the physician's PHS, which resulted in misidentification at a rate of 6% ± 9. The automatic location determination engine and information on PHS location are complementary, and using the two in combination improved accuracy. This information was used to regulate the system, *e.g.*, vocal warnings sent while the physician was seeing outpatients were switched to text messages.

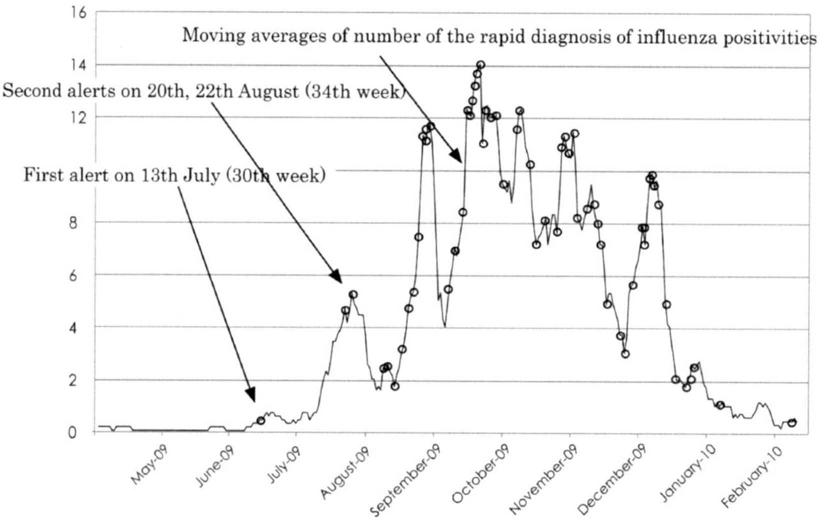

Figure 6: Outbreaks of the H1N1 influenza pandemic that occurred in summer 2009.

4. DISCUSSION

Computerized physician order entry (CPOE) systems with clinical decision support software are widely viewed as crucial for reducing medical errors and saving costs [10-20]. However, clinicians disregard alerts from CDS a majority of the time. Sometimes, alerts are ignored due to "alert fatigue". In other cases, clinicians prefer to rely on their own judgment [21,22]. There is concern that the low signal-to-noise ratio of alerting systems can desensitize users to all alerts, which may result in important alerts being ignored or missed. An additional concern is that the amount of time devoted to unnecessary alerts is a lost opportunity to focus on more important patient care issues [23]. The results of this study show that the encouragement of team care by CDSS and high signal-to-noise rate were effective at accepting alerts.

4.1. Real Time or Retrospective

When clinicians use EMR with CDSS capabilities to assist in real-time decision-making, patient care is improved. And when clinicians, administrators, and researchers use such systems for decision-making, patient care is further improved [24]. Fig. (**7**), a former comprehensive CDS requires analytical data processing at both the transactional and aggregate levels. One is transactional data acquired by their EMR to support real-time transactional, patient-based clinical care processing with On-line transactional processing (OLTP).

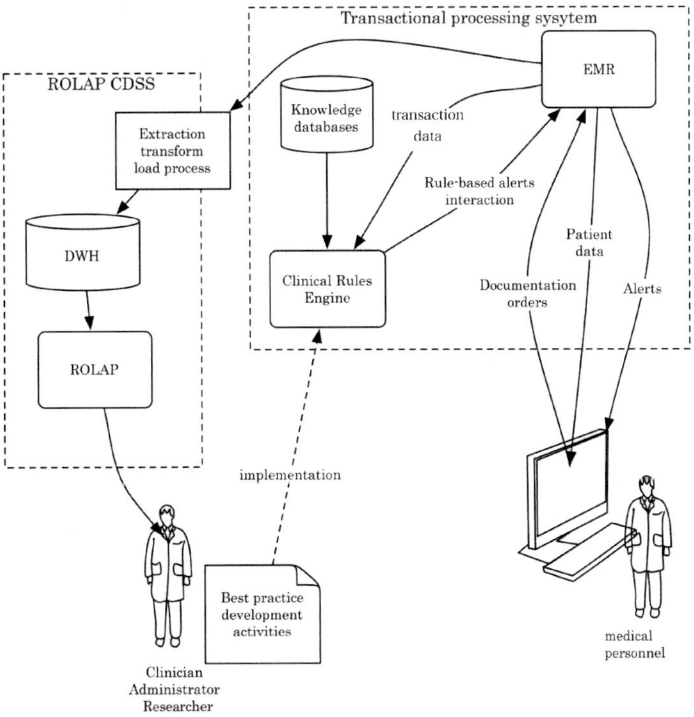

Figure 7: A former CDSS with OLTP and ROLAP.

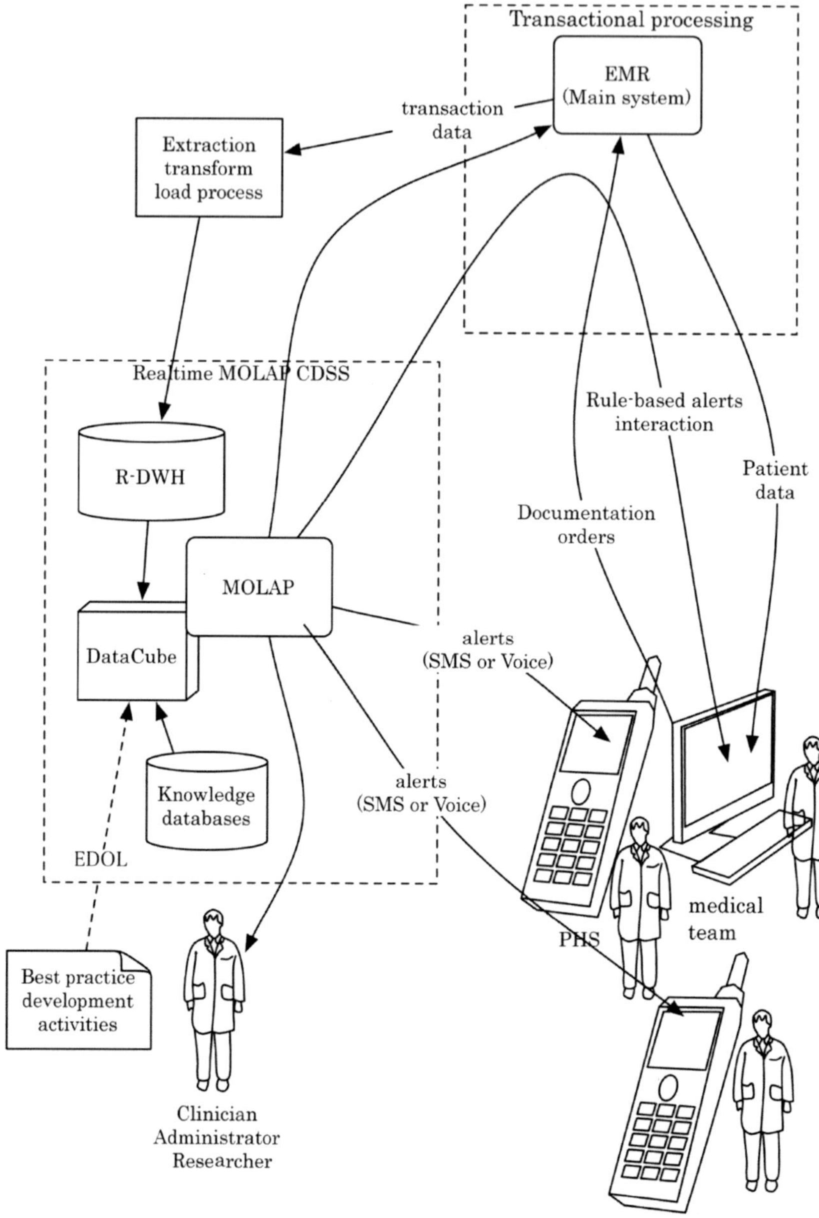

Figure 8: HiPER 2.0 with Real-time DWH and MOLAP.

The other is retrospective, population-based aggregate analysis with on-line analytical processing (OLAP). However, Fig. (**8**) HiPER 2.0 used real-time DWH and OLAP, thus provided facilities for patient-focused, point-of-care OLAP and also aggregate, multidimensional analysis with the use of the latest data.

4.2. MOLAP and ROLAP

Relational OLAP (ROLAP) or multi-dimensional OLAP (MOLAP) can implement OLAP for a DWH. ROLAP depends on queries that drill into a relational database (RDB). HiPER 2.0 includes vertically integrated storage with information that is not indexed and with limited queries, so drilling into a RDB is not feasible. Thus, MOLAP is used on the server, and data cubes are mixed in with a RDB. Both parallel and real-time processing are provided by implementing the ETL process from the main system to the DWH, while building data cubes and also featuring an EDOL interpreter in the same stream to intelligently process those cubes.

4.3. An Automatic Syndromic Surveillance System

Syndrome classification is one of the first and important steps in syndromic data processing and analysis. The syndrome classification process can be implemented either as a manual process or through an automated system. Chief complaints from patient encounters are collected more often as free texts (70%) than in ICD-9 coded formats (30%), which may suggest the importance of natural language processing techniques for medical information processing in this area [8]. For instance, ICD-9–coded emergency department (ED) diagnoses and free-text triage diagnoses are routinely collected data elements that have potential value for public health epidemics. Experiments comparing two Bayesian classifiers for the acute gastrointestinal syndrome showed only 68 percent mapping success against expert classification of ED reports [25].

We do not implement the syndrome classification process and can identify the target syndrome from natural sentences with high accuracy. Thus, we developed an anomalous pattern detection method similar to WSARE instead of syndrome classification process. The What's Strange About Recent Events (WSARE) algorithm detects anomalous patterns in discrete, multidimensional data sets with a temporal component [26]. WSARE, searching for groups with specific characteristics, for example a recent pattern of place, age, and diagnosis associated with illness that is anomalous when compared with historic patterns. In contrast, we only used syndrome patterns. Specificity and positive predictive value were 96.7% and 90.3%, respectively. These values were high level, thus we can detect an unusual outbreak of the H1N1 influenza pandemic that occurred in summer 2009. We have shown that data from syndrome pattern can provide low cost and timely ILI surveillance throughout the year.

4.4. Purpose of CDSS

The reason for using a CDSS is to improve the process of providing medical care, but whether the care provided is best suited to the individual patient and whether the care is provided efficiently to a group of patients are questions that the clinician must answer in accordance with the conditions. The one who makes decisions and assumes responsibility for that decision is the physician, therefore, a CDSS merely assists the clinician in making a decision and should not make decisions in place of the clinician. In addition, non-specialists must avoid the incorrect decisions from the CDSS.

Man and conditions determine human behavior. Humans project those conditions into psychological space and in that space act rationally and correctly within their realm of understanding. The risk in medical care comes from the failure to project conditions with no goals of an action in mind. Conditions in medical care are such that much work is left unfinished, circumstances differ with the individual, time tends to be constrained, varied types of information are available, there are always irregularities, substantial strain is intensified, and standardization comes too late. Human reliability suffers particularly during emergencies. Thus, to compensate for human failings, a CDSS that aids in projecting conditions into psychological space will lead to less risk.

Care settings are host to a number of electronic devices and person-to-person interfaces like communication devices. Thus, interfaces play a major role in projecting the clinician into psychological space. Professionals like clinicians need interfaces with the ability to list information and will even tolerate complex lists. In addition, the best interface will probably differ for each individual. Looking at the processing of medical information from the perspective of cognitive science reveals that one's level of proficiency at specialized skills is not simply proportional to time; there are variations in the accuracy of operation and level of understanding for personnel with different levels of proficiency and in different occupations. In addition, which interface is best differs for interface designers and users, leading to a variety of interfaces.

The conventional interface for a CDSS is a screen showing electronic medical records, so its focus is on visual presentation. Modern humans read in characteristic formats that emphasize continuity, coherence, or uniformity; humans tend to discern a continuum of information linearly. When information that will serve as the basis for a decision is simply listed or displayed after a certain set of operations, re-arrangement of that information so that it can be discerned linearly depends on the qualities of the individual and carries the risk of failing to project that information into psychological space. Thus, re-arranging information and manipulating it to make it easier for the clinician to discern linearly helped the CDSS to project that information into psychological space. Moreover, using visual as well as auditory cues in the interface has changed the current reality in which individuals resort to visual cues.

Depending on the clinician, the information may have already been mapped to psychological space as that might invite risk, if the clinician has preconceptions beyond the information displayed. Thus, providing information to make a decision to relevant parties with few preconceptions and encouraging consultation with the clinician may further reduced the risk.

To sum up, a feature that a CDSS needs to have is the ability to locate relevant parties in a timely manner. A conventional system that follows only the patient's viewpoint is incapable of this. This is now possible with a CDSS, which can ascertain how experienced medical personnel are, what they know, and what they do not know. The highligted sentences are two contradictory statements which produces ambiguity regarding the CDSS system. In the process of providing medical care, the support provided by a CDSS allows one to discern "under what conditions (the impetus)" "someone (an intervening party)" "will affect (the effect of that intervention)" "someone else (the individual affected by that intervention)". With respect to problematic actions and results as defined within the process of providing medical care, the frequency with which an individual intervenes will change depending on how busy the individual is and the work the individual must do. The physical and philosophical state of medical personnel must be determined to identify intervening individuals. Individuals planning medical care or providing that care should be followed to identify the individuals affected by intervention. A plan to linearly map information an intervening individual needs to make a decision must be prepared beforehand, though these plans will change dynamically depending on the experience and status of the intervening individual.

The process by which medical care was provided was gauged, information, including that on planned medical care, was collected, and the behavior of medical personnel was analyzed. Cell phones were used to fashion a system linked to those medical personnel that allowed information to be disseminated under any circumstances. Information on medical care in actual practice was instantaneously digitized and then a CDSS was reconfigured as a series of systems featuring speech synthesis and controlling a switchboard to implement HiPER 2.0. HiPER 2.0 is limited to displaying information and does not make decisions. Decisions are made by medical personnel, and actual decisions are the result of discussions among medical personnel.

Discovering problematic actions and results in the process of medical care may lead to doubts as to whether the system is conducive to medical decisions. The threshold for selecting which information to display changes dynamically depending on the level of experience and status of the recipient of that information. As an example, a great deal of information may be shown to an expert. Here, HiPER 2.0 prompted consultation, but the decision on whether or not to actually consult someone else was left to medical personnel. However, if information is not disclosed then it does not exist for medical personnel. If HiPER 2.0 controls the level of information disclosed and how accessible it is, then HiPER 2.0 may have been deciding how that information was disclosed. Many of the decision thresholds incorporated in conventional CDSSes are determined by absolute rules based on society or hospital guidelines or experience. However, conditions for patients vary, and determining absolute rules with respect to often-changing conditions for medical personnel is difficult. The individual focus of both the patient and medical personnel could be identified based on the notes and actions from medical personnel. In other words, the level of information disclosed must be defined while keeping in mind how busy medical personnel are and what their focus is. The definition of the level of information to disclose is a set of individual thresholds, but if information is stored individually in abstract form, it can be searched, classified, and re-used when similar circumstances occur. Modification and development of conventional interfaces lend itself to better projection of information stored on a machine into the psychological space of humans. In contrast, the new CDSS cited here created a virtual space within the CDSS to take the place of the psychological space in humans, and this CDSS was used to re-define the level of information to disclose. Definitions of the level of information to disclose have been bandied about by a number of medical personnel, and interfaces with enhanced "awareness" may alter views on CDSSes and allow humans to better coexist with them.

CONFLICT OF INTEREST

None declared.

ACKNOWLEDGEMENT

None declared.

REFERENCES

[1] Mollon B, Chong JJ, Holbrook AM, Sung M, Thabane L, Foster G. Features predicting the success of computerized decision support for prescribing: a systematic review of randomized controlled trials. BMC Med Inform Decis Mak 2009; 9(1): 11.

[2] Pearson SA, Moxey A, Robertson J, *et al.* Do computerised clinical decision support systems for prescribing change practice? A systematicreviewoftheliterature(1990-2007). BMC Health Serv Res 2009; 9(1): 154.

[3] Kawamoto K, Houlihan CA, Balas EA, Lobach DF. Improving clinical practice using clinical decision support systems: a systematic review of trials to identify features critical to success. Bmj 2005; 330(7494): 765.

[4] Hunt DL, Haynes RB, Hanna SE, Smith K. Effects of computer-based clinical decision support systems on physician performance and patient outcomes: a systematic review. JAMA 1998; 280(15): 1339-46.

[5] Garg AX, Adhikari NKJ, McDonald H, *et al.* Effects of computerized clinical decision support systems on practitioner performance and patient outcomes. A systematic review. JAMA 2005; 293: 1223-38.

[6] Gilbert S, Lynch N. Brewer's conjecture and the feasibility of consistent, available, partition-tolerant web services. ACM SIGACT, New Volume 33; Issue 2: 51-59.

[7] Heffernan R, Mostashari F, Das D, Karpati A, Kulldorff M, Weiss D. Syndromic surveillance in public health practice, New York City. Emerg Infect Dis 2004; 10(5): 858-64.

[8] Yan P *et al.*, Syndromic surveillance systems. Public health and biodefense. Annu Rev Inform Sci Tech 42, 2008

[9] Buehler, J., Berkelman, R., Hartley, D., Peters, C. (2003). Syndromic Surveillance and Bioterrorism-related Epidemics. Emerg Infect Dis 2003; 9(1), 197-204.

[10] Raebel MA, Carroll NM, Kelleher JA, *et al.* Randomized trial to improve prescribing safety during Pregnancy. J Am Med Inform Assoc 2007; 14:440 – 50.

[11] Berner ES, Houston TK, Ray MN, *et al.* Improving ambulatory prescribing safety with a handheld decision support system: a randomized controlled trial. J Am Med Inform Assoc 2006; 13: 171-79.

[12] Javitt JC, Steinberg G, Locke T, *et al.* Using a claims data-based sentinel system to improve compliance with clinical guidelines: results of a randomized prospective study. Am J Manag Care 2005; 11: 93-102.

[13] Blendon RJ, DesRoches CM, Brodie M, *et al.* Views of practicing physicians and the public on medical errors. N Engl J Med 2003; 347: 1933-67.

[14] Tamblyn R, Huang A, Perreault R, *et al.* The medical office of the 21st century (MOXXI): effectiveness of computerized decision-making support in reducing inappropriate prescribing in primary care. CMAJ 2003; 169: 549-56.

[15] Bates DW, Gawande AA. Patient safety: improving safety with information technology. N Engl J Med 2003; 348: 2526-34.

[16] Bates DW, Cohen M, Leape LL, Overhage JM, Shabot MM, Sheridan T. Reducing the frequency of errors in medicine using information technology. J Am Med Inform Assoc 2001; 8:299-308.

[17] Kohn LT, Corrigan J, Donaldson MS, Eds. To Err Is Human: Building a Safer Health System. Washing- ton, DC: National Academy Press, 2000.

[18] Teich JM, Merchia PR, Schmiz JL, *et al.* Effects of computerized physician order entry on prescribing practices. Arch Intern Med 2000; 160: 2741-47.

[19] BatesDW, LeapeLL, CullenDJ, *et al.* Effect of computerized physician order entry and a team intervention on prevention of serious medication errors. JAMA 1998; 280: 1311-16.

[20] Sittig DF, Stead WW. Computer-based physician order entry: the state of the art. J Am Med In form Assoc 1994; 1: 108-23.

[21] William LG, Robert JD, Audrius P. A Trial of Automated Decision Support Alerts for Contraindicated Medications Using Computerized Physician Order Entry. J Am Med Inform Assoc 2005; 12(3): 269-74.

[22] Thomas I, Joel SW, Roger BD, *et al.* Overrides of Medication Alerts in Ambulatory.Arch Intern Med 2009; 169(3): 305-11.

[23] Ko Y, Abarca J, Malone DC, *et al.* Practitioners' views on computerized drug-drug interaction alerts in the VA system. J Am Med Inform Assoc 2007; 14 (1): 56-64

[24] Ledbetter CS, Morgan MW. Toward best practice: Leveraging the electronic patient record as a clinical data warehouse. J Healthcare Info Manage 2001; 15(2): 119-31

[25] Ivanov, O, Wagner, MM, Chapman, WW, Olszewski RT. Accuracy of Three Classifiers of Acute Gastrointestinal Syndrome for Syndromic Surveillance. In Proceedings of the AMIA Symp, San Antonio: USA 2002; pp. 345-49.

[26] Kaufman Z, Wong WK, Peled-Leviatan T, *et al.* Evaluation of a syndromic surveillance system using the WSARE algorithm for early detection of an unusual, localized summer outbreak of influenza B: implications for bioterrorism surveillance. Isr Med Assoc J 2007; 9(1): 3-7.

CHAPTER 3

Bi-Directional Integration Between EMR and FileMaker

Shigeru Yoshida*

Nagoya University Hospital, 65 Tsurumai, Showa-Ku, Nagoya, Aichi, Japan

Abstract: We developed end-user computing solutions with FileMaker. In addition, we successfully built a bidirectional integration scheme between our electronic medical records (EMR) system and the FileMaker solutions. The key to success is that we built a simple integration scheme and divided responsibility in case of problems between the EMR system and the FileMaker solutions.

Keywords: EMR, FileMaker Pro, Integration, Cooperation, Bi-directional, User-made, EUC, J-SUMMITS, NeoChart, CSV, XML, DDE command, FileMaker portal, Forest, CDSS, iPad.

1. INTRODUCTION

Nagoya University Hospital is one of the largest hospitals in Japan, and is a core medical facility in central Japan. We have more than 1000 hospital beds, more than 2000 outpatient visits per day, and perform approximately 10000 operations per year.

We have been operating an electronic medical records (EMR) system developed by Fujitsu since 2002, and also have an end-user computing (EUC) system developed in FileMaker. These systems complement each other and there is bidirectional integration between the EMR and the FileMaker solutions [1].

We describe the integration scheme in this chapter.

2. METHODS

The FileMaker solutions were introduced in 2007 at Nagoya University Hospital, which has 33 departments, 1035 beds, 500 doctors, and 850 nurses.

***Address correspondence to Shigeru Yoshida:** Medical IT Center, Nagoya University Hospital, Japan; E-mail: shigeru@med.nagoya-u.ac.jp

2.1. EMR Configuration

First, we describe the entire system configuration of our EMR called NeoChart. This is a client–server system including PRIMEQUEST 580 with the 64-bit Red Hat Enterprise Linux operating system and 32 (64 core) Intel Itanium processors. We have adopted Caché as backend, which is an object-oriented Database Management System (DBMS). We have approximately 1000 Desktop PCs, 350 laptop PCs, and 350 PDAs. The operating system (OS) of all the clients PCs is Windows XP. We have achieved paperless and filmless operation, and X-ray, laboratory results, ECG, EEG, and all systems including the FileMaker solutions are connected to the EMR system.

2.2. FileMaker Solutions Configuration

The configuration of the FileMaker solutions is described below.

We have one FileMaker server and 1000 client PCs. The server application version is FileMaker Server 8 and the client application version is FileMaker Pro 8.5. The FileMaker Server 8 works on Windows Server 2003 R2 and the client FileMaker Pro 8.5 works on Windows XP. The FileMaker Server hosts 61 files.

2.3. Authentication

How our FileMaker solutions work on the client PC is described here in detail. We adopted fingerprint authentication to ensure reliability of our EMR system. After logging into the EMR, we can start the FileMaker Navigation Portal from one of the EMR launcher menus. There are functional restrictions in the Windows OS and applications on the client PC in that there is no way to run FileMaker except *via* the EMR. That is, we cannot run FileMaker solutions without authentication by the EMR. Thus, strict authentication is achieved, which is a weak point of FileMaker.

2.4. Startup Process (Fig. 1)

A CSV file containing user ID, patient ID, and additional data, if needed is exported to the local folder. When we start a FileMaker solution, all data must be present. Then, a startup script of the FileMaker solution executes and imports the contents of the CSV file, and finally the CSV file is deleted by the FileMaker

DDE command. Thus, the appropriate data are transferred from EMR system to the FileMaker solution for the purpose of identification of records.

2.5. Background Processes (Fig. 2)

We have many FileMaker solutions on the Navigation Portal, *e.g.*, an infection control system, a reservation system, a bed control system, *etc.* These are described in detail later.

When we use these systems, large amounts of information on the EMR system are required, such as patient information, prescription information, and laboratory results. Therefore, we made a background coordination scheme between the EMR server and the FileMaker server. That is, the patient information table of the EMR system is regularly exported as a CSV file from the EMR server and is imported into the FileMaker server automatically every 6 minutes.

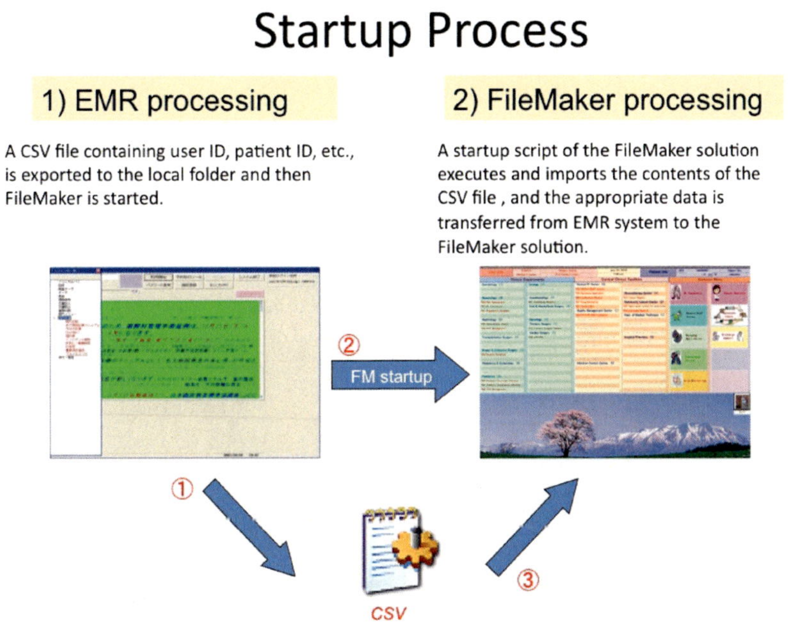

Figure 1: Startup coordination scheme.

A CSV file containing user ID, patient ID, *etc.*, is exported to the local folder when FileMaker is started.

Other tables are coordinated in the same way at appropriate intervals. Each interval is as follows.

The prescription information table is updated every 6 minutes, the diagnosis table and the laboratory results table are updated once in an hour, and the user information table, the surgical information table, the reference information table, and the physiological data table are updated once a day.

As a result, we can get a lot of information from the EMR system by entering user ID, patient ID, *etc.* This integration scheme is very simple, so specialized skills and knowledge of database connectivity, such as ODBC, are not required. Another advantage of this scheme is that it is easy to divide responsibility between the EMR system and the FileMaker solutions in the case of problems. As our FileMaker solutions do not actually access the tables of the EMR system, they do not affect the EMR operation. This is very important in building a coordination scheme with EMR vendors. Most of these vendors do not like to build complicated integration schemes between their EMR system and EUC system, such as FileMaker solutions as they do not wish to be liable for problems due to EUC system failure.

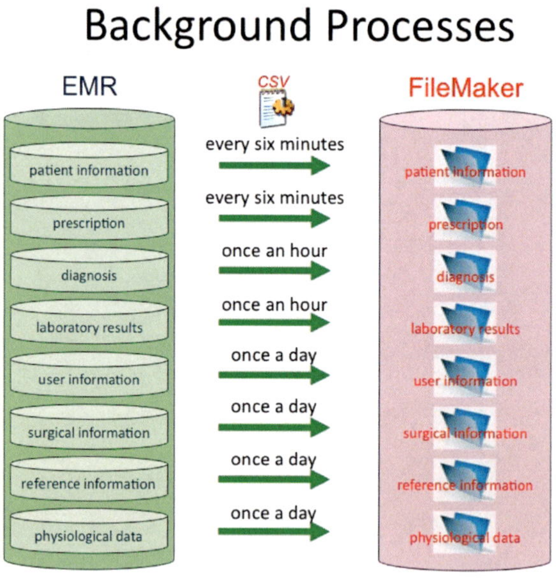

Figure 2: Background integration processes.

2.6. From FileMaker Solutions to the EMR System (Fig. 3)

Our fundamental definition of the FileMaker solutions is that it is not a legal medical records system but a support system. Therefore, it is necessary to write certain information from our FileMaker solutions to the EMR system defined as legal medical records if necessary. The method is as follows.

When a FileMaker solution runs according to the startup process described above, a resident program named CTFM2000 runs concurrently. It is on standby while the FileMaker solution is running and becomes activated when the FileMaker solution must write data into the EMR system, and after writing it returns to the standby state. The practical procedure of data writing is as follows.

When we need to write some data from a FileMaker database into the EMR system as part of legal medical records, we run a script in FileMaker purpose of which is to export the data in XML format in the local folder and it sends the message as a DDE command to CTFM2000. After receiving the message, the dialog box of the CTFM2000 is activated and we can verify the data in user-friendly text format.

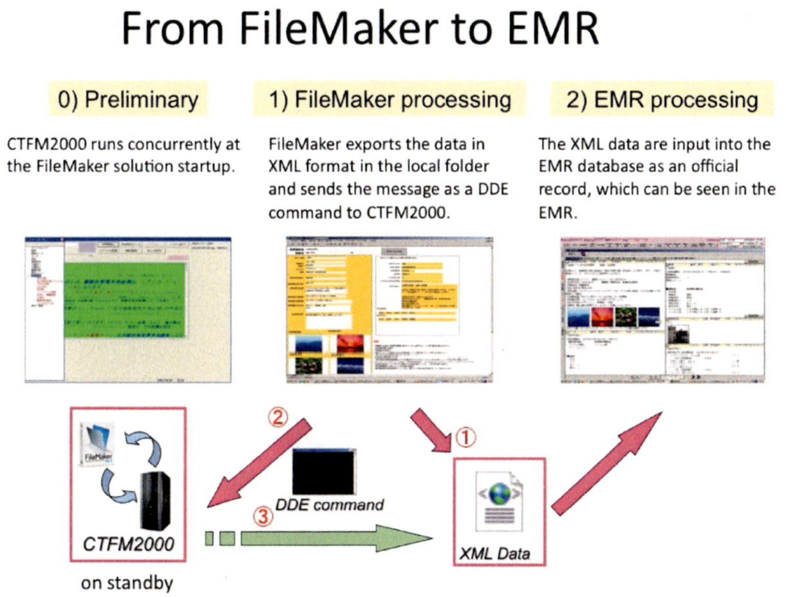

Figure 3: Scheme of sending XML data from FileMaker to EMR.

Finally, we perform the procedure and the XML data exported from the FileMaker database are fed into the EMR database as a legal medical record. The record can be viewed completely like any other record in EMR. CTFM2000 recognizes the user ID, patient ID, FileMaker database ID, and record ID when feeding the data into the EMR.

CTFM2000 runs concurrently at the FileMaker solution startup.

FileMaker exports the data in XML format in the local folder and sends the message as a DDE command to CTFM2000.

The XML data are fed into the EMR database as an official record, which can be seen in the EMR.

If the patient ID is different between the sent data and EMR database, even though they are usually identical, CTFM2000 sends an alert and the data are not fed into the EMR. If the data are changed on the FileMaker database and fed into the EMR database again, the EMR system recognizes the consistency of the patient ID, the FileMaker database ID, and the record ID, and judges that the record is revised. The record is then made as the latest revision in the EMR database. Of course, we can read all versions of the record. That is, perfect revision control by the EMR system is performed. The FileMaker solution is not good at revision control and it is very difficult to achieve perfect revision control using the FileMaker solution alone. This is a great advantage of this method. Furthermore, we can send various other types of information rather than solely relying on text format. Image information, such as a JPEG or PDF formats, can be sent to EMR as file attachments. Therefore, we can send a printed image of a document made by the FileMaker solution.

We can send account information to the hospital accounting system through the EMR system just by adding an one-line message to the sent data. The important thing is that this program (CTFM2000) was built by the EMR vendor. Not only sending the data to the EMR system but also writing the data into the EMR database directly represent great risks for the EMR vendor, so they are unlikely to allow us to do so in our own way. In our case, we left the procedure to the EMR vendors, and they were willing to work out the details. This is the key to success. The integration scheme described above enables us to use the FileMaker solutions effectively and efficiently in integration with the EMR system.

3. RESULTS

3.1. FileMaker Contents

We operate about seventy FileMaker solutions effectively. Some of the representative solutions are described below.

3.2. The Navigation Portal (F001) (Fig.4)

The Navigation Portal (F001) (Fig. **4**) is a portal solution for all of the FileMaker solutions. It has many title buttons to open each solution.

Figure 4: The Navigation Portal (F001).

As mentioned above, all of the FileMaker solutions can be started only by opening this portal solution from the launcher menu of EMR.

The user ID is imported from EMR and displayed with the user name and other attributes at the top left of the screen. The patient ID is also imported and displayed with the patient name and other attributes in the top right of the screen. After opening this portal file, we can select and open each FileMaker solution by clicking the title. When we open a solution, the user information and the patient information are transferred to the solution and always displayed on the top of the screen. In fact, we can open each FileMaker solution directly from each launcher menu of EMR, but even then the Navigation Portal (F001) is opened in the background before opening each FileMaker solution and the user information and the patient information are transferred. When we close each FileMaker solution, we can either quit or return to the Navigation Portal (F001).

3.3. Community Liaison Reservation (F002) (Fig. 5)

The community liaison reservation (F002) (Fig. **5**) enables collaborating doctors to make reservations for imaging tests for their patients by phone.

Figure 5: Reservation system for the community.

When the operator in the regional collaborating center receives a phone call from a collaborating doctor, this solution is accessed to find time for imaging tests, such as CT, MRI, PET, and mammography at the doctor's request. It is very easy to use because the operator simply inputs the phone number of the doctor and the patient ID, and then a few clicks to choose the time.

We operate several reservation systems developed in FileMaker other than F002. For example, a reservation system for urology OPD (F017), a reservation system for in-house workshop (F024), a reservation system for immunization program (F038), and a dialysis center reservation system (F042), *etc.*

3.4. Cancer Registration (F014) (Fig. 6)

Cancer registration (F014) (Fig. **6**) registers all the cancer patients in our hospital to allow reporting to the government. The format of F014 is set up in the same way as the official cancer registration system. Therefore, it is very easy to import the data from F014 into the official database.

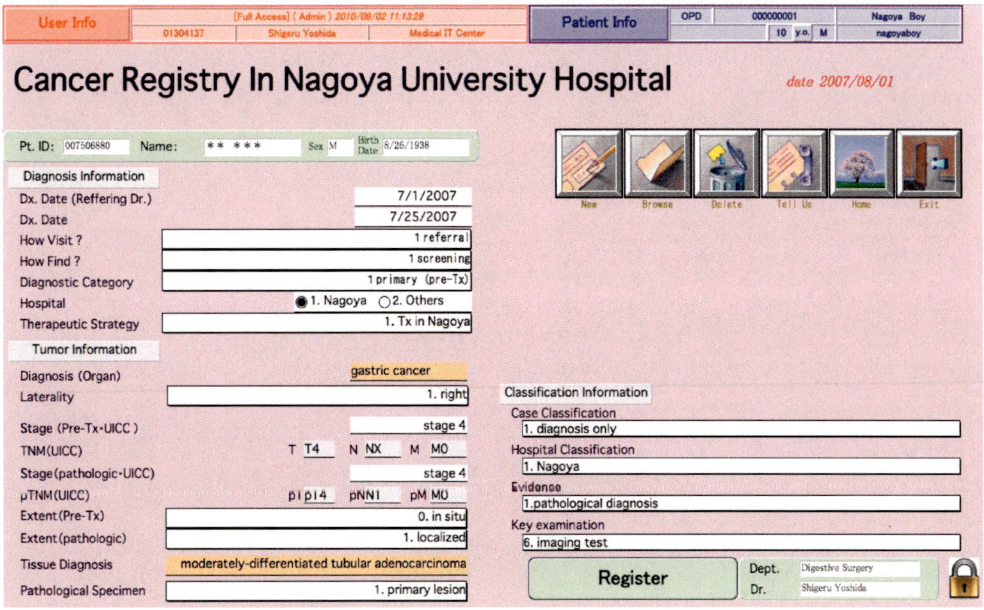

Figure 6: Cancer registration system.

We can easily obtain much of the information required for cancer registration and can also find new cancer patients using this system. Without F014, we would have difficulty reporting to the government. We would have to input large amounts of data manually into the official cancer registration system, and it would take a great deal of time and energy to identify new cancer patients.

We have four more registration systems compatible with each official system as well as F014, *i.e.*, Japan EPINet registration system (F016), Anesthesia case management system (F021), and JACVSD (F036), which is our FileMaker version of the Japan Adult Cardiovascular Surgery Database.

3.5. Case Management System for Thoracic Surgery (F018) (Fig. 7)

The case management system for thoracic surgery (F018) (Fig. **7**) was developed by one of the thoracic surgeons in our hospital. This system can be used to manage all of the thoracic surgery patients, each disease, and each surgery. All tables, layouts, and functions of this database are optimized for daily practice and research regarding thoracic surgery because the author is familiar with all of these and has actual experience of using the system.

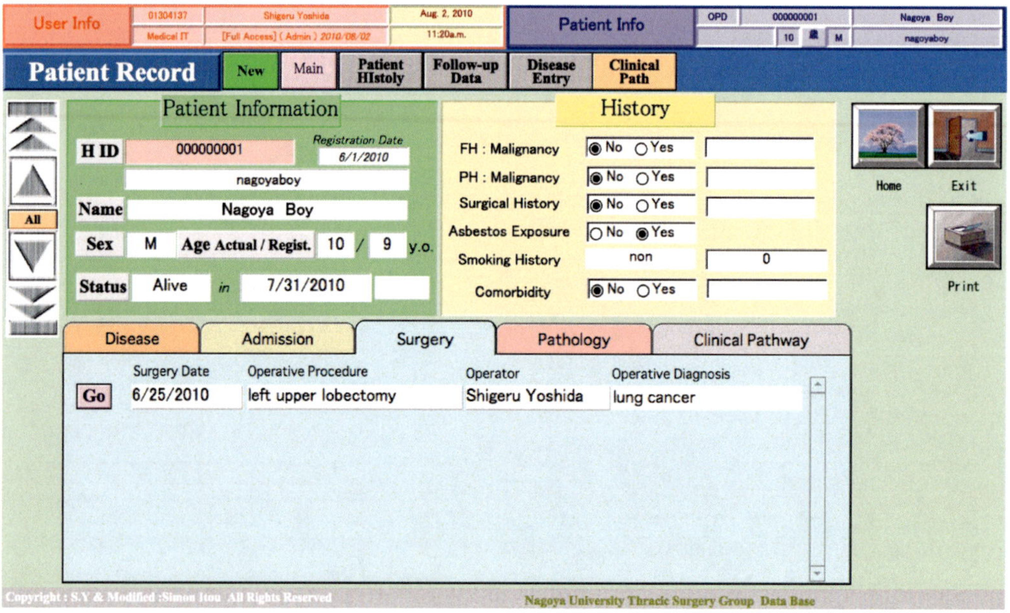

Figure 7: Case management system for thoracic surgery.

We operate various disease databases, such as blood disease (F004), live liver transplantation (F020), pediatric disease (F030, F031, F033, F052), gynecological disease (F039, F040, F045), respiratory disease (F041), chronic kidney disease (F046), and dental disease (F049, F050) databases. Each database was developed or designed by a specialist in the disease, which makes it both high in quality as well as easy to use.

Renal biopsy report (F035) is a simple format database that was developed mainly for the creation and printing of reports. This type of FileMaker database is commonly used among general users because it is not difficult to make a simple report using FileMaker; a small amount of training enables them to make such a report of database useful for their own work.

3.6. DVT/PE Risk Evaluation System (F048) (Fig. 8)

DVT/PE risk evaluation system (F048) (Fig. **8**) is a Clinical Decision Support System (CDSS). Deep vein thrombosis (DVT) and pulmonary embolism (PE) are major complications during hospitalization in both surgery and non-surgery patients. Prevention of these complications is very important, and therefore detailed knowledge and specialized judgment are required. F048 assists doctors to perform the optimal prevention method. The procedure is as follows.

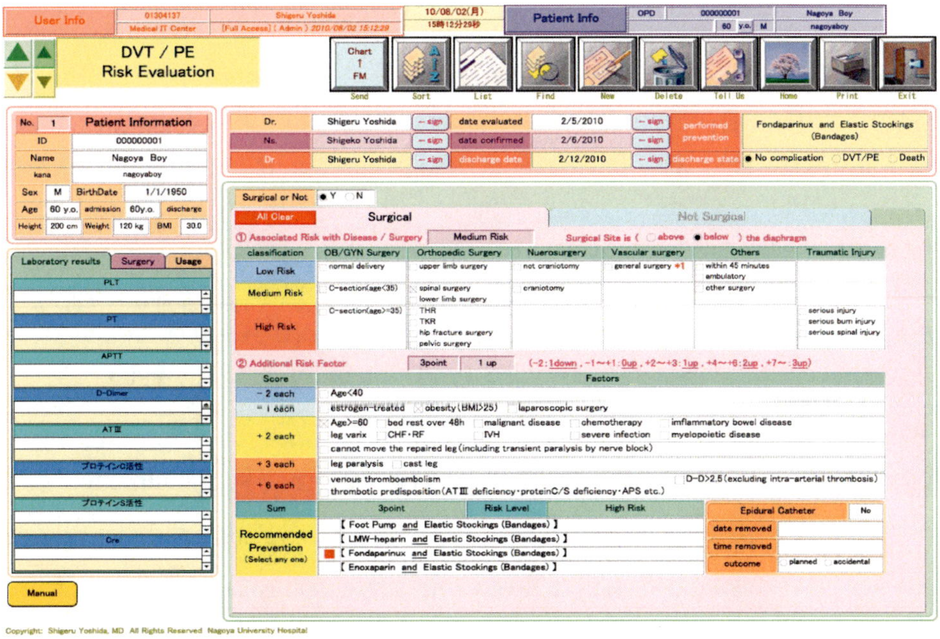

Figure 8: DVT/PE risk evaluation system.

First, we select whether the patient is surgical or non-surgical, and evaluate the risk associated with the disease or surgery, and then a tentative risk level is displayed. Second, we check the additional risk factor, and then the final risk level is determined and several recommended preventive measures are presented. Finally, we select and perform one of these methods.

The medical contents of F048 were created after extensive discussions with an expert committee. As a member of the committee, I found this solution through these discussions.

It would not have been possible for non-medical personnel to have built this database simultaneously with the discussions in these committees.

We have another CDSS like F048 called Mr. Pneumonia (F037), which provides precise advice regarding pneumonia treatment. This is because F037 was developed by a physician specializing in respiratory infection based on his abundant experience and high-quality evidence regarding pneumonia treatment. We input some information about the patient, and it shows the appropriate therapeutic approach. F037 has been adopted in some affiliated hospitals, and a multicenter study using F037 will be conducted in the near future.

4. DISCUSSION

All of the FileMaker solutions are built by users themselves and they are successfully integrated with the EMR system bi-directionally [2]. Until recently, it was not possible to securely manage these FileMaker solutions. They have been used on private PCs in the doctors' offices. As they were made and managed by doctors, they could not be sufficiently controlled. There was no integration between the FileMaker solutions and the EMR system. Therefore, it was very inconvenient for users to reenter the data already present in EMR into FileMaker again.

We planned to manage the FileMaker solutions by ourselves and integrate them with the EMR system to achieve both improved security and convenience.

The first step in our plan was a questionnaire survey regarding FileMaker usage. More than 30 departments responded to this survey, and the results showed that FileMaker databases were used in approximately 80% of the departments in our hospital.

The survey also showed that most doctors wanted their databases to be managed by our IT department. Indeed, they were anxious about information security.

The next step was to agree with the EMR vendor on integration with the FileMaker solutions. We were careful to avoid complicated structures and to ensure there were no adverse effects on the mission-critical EMR system. As a result, the integration scheme was superficial and loose, as mentioned above. The agreement of the EMR vendor may not have been obtained if we had demanded closer integration, including direct access to the EMR system.

The final stages of the integration plan are still in progress. We are trying to incorporate the FileMaker solutions into the electronic clinical pathway system. We are also preparing to implement the FileMaker solutions on portable devices, such as the iPad.

As described above, our FileMaker solutions are convenient and easy to use because they are developed by medical doctors who actually operate them and who best know their own practices. There is no staff capable of making the specifications of the system in most hospitals in Japan, and healthcare workers such as medical doctors often have to talk directly with system engineers. This is one of the greatest problems in the construction of medical IT systems in Japan. The healthcare workers alone are not able to successfully communicate their demands to the system engineers of the IT vendor.

In many cases, the system is not completed as expected and they feel dissatisfied from it.

This is also suboptimal for the vendor's programmers. Making a system without good specifications takes a great deal of time and energy, and it can be very stressful coping with user dissatisfaction. Therefore, we decided to implement the FileMaker solutions as EUC designed to integrate with the EMR system to resolve these problems. This yielded three benefits.

1. It was possible to manage the FileMaker databases that have been used on private PCs in the doctors' offices by consolidating them into our server. This results in a marked improvement in information security.

2. We were able to save both cost and time, which were well received by the management.

3. It became possible to respond to corrections and additions quickly, which increased user satisfaction.

According to the result of a questionnaire survey at a symposium, approximately one third of the attendants have the FileMaker solutions in their hospitals. Although this may be specific for Japan, medical doctors are generally good at developing databases in FileMaker. In fact, many doctors develop FileMaker databases for their daily work.

In 2008, we started an organization called the Japanese Society for User-Made Medical IT System (J-SUMMITS). "User-made" means developed not by programmers but by the users themselves. It means end-user computing.

J-SUMMITS now has over 300 members. There are dozens of hospitals where the FileMaker solutions as the EUC are integrated with the EMR system. Some have different means of integration, as described in other chapters.

At the end of this chapter, we emphasize that our greatest goal is to improve the quality of medical care.

CONFLICT OF INTEREST

None declared.

ACKNOWLEDGEMENT

None declared.

REFERENCES

[1] Yoshida S. Utility of software developed with FileMaker Pro in Japanese medical field. Conference Book of International Conference on Complex Medical Engineering, Beijing: China, pp. 279-282.

[2] Yoshida S. Matsunami K, Okagaki K, *et al*. Intersystem coordination between EMR and user-made system. Japan Journal of Medical Informatis 2009; 29(Suppl): 268-273.

CHAPTER 4

Document-Oriented Computing-Based System

Akira Ohtahara*

San-in Rosai Hospital, 1-8-1 Kaike-Shinden, Yonago, Tottori, Japan

Abstract: This was a record for introduction of a fusion (document-oriented, computing-based) system which supports EMR (EMR) system by using FileMaker Pro Ver. 9 server, for changing a paper-based system in our hospital. For this purpose an End User Computing (EUC) strategy was taken to train and encourage the front-end users involved in the development of applications. Many documents which were made by the FileMaker Pro system were kept in PDF format on the EMR server. One advantage of this system was the similarity about end user's tasks for filling up these documents with the past paper-based system. End users suffered less from disorientation and misunderstanding. Another advantage was that easy negotiation between each section was re-examined in regard to site needs or job alternation as with the PDCA cycle approach. However, differences in the levels of various applications and variations in operating environments seem to have given rise to a number of problems. In addition, there have also been issues with application maintenance when the person in charge resigns.

Keywords: EMR, FileMaker Pro, Document-oriented, PDF, QR code, EUC, PDCA cycle, SQL, CSV, ESS, power-user group, user's task, workflow, data flow process.

1. INTRODUCTION

Computer-based processing and storage systems in hospitals offer the advantages of allowing information resources to be saved, searched and interconnected more than with paper-based systems. In recent years, hospital information systems have spread not only to large-scale urban hospitals but also to local and small-scale medical facilities and doctor's offices. On the other hand, paper-based document systems in hospitals are advantageous in that they allow easy carrying, grouping with accompanying documents and the affixation of signatures. Even if a huge integrated computing system was constructed in a specific hospital, it might be

***Address correspondence to Akira Ohtahara:** Division of Cardiology, San-in Rosai Hospital, Japan; E-mail: ohtahara@saninh.rofuku.go.jp

Shunji Wakamiya, Kazunobu Yamauchi and Hiroyuki Yoshihara (Eds)

expensive and complicated to perform all the necessary functions without any paper documentation whatsoever. This was a necessary consideration in the success introduction of a fusion (document-oriented, computing-based) system from a paper-based system in our hospital.

2. METHOD

2.1. Planning with an End User Computing (EUC) Strategy

Unfortunately, there was only a short preparation period of six months in which we had to build our fusion system due to the late decision to change the hospital's setup from an ordering system to an electronic chart system. Previously, a paper-based approach (other than for some back-office operations) had mainly been used in the hospital, and adopting a computer-based system within a short space of time posed a number of serious challenges. Considering the respective advantages of computer-based and paper-based systems, we chose an EUC strategy to train and encourage the front-end users involved in the development of applications [1]. To enable output of the huge amounts of paper documentation used in many duties for all faculty members (doctors, nurses, technicians, dieticians, clerks, *etc.,*) the FileMaker Pro Ver. 9 server client computer system was selected for its easy operation and versatility. The vendors also supported the FileMaker Pro Ver. 9 server client computer system for making documents with their EMR system. Fortunately, some faculty members in each section had used this software before.

These individuals were selected as power-users for developing applications to make documents in each section. To support them, an intensive course on FileMaker Pro application development was given in advance, and a temporary tutor was employed for this purpose. To maintain quality control in application development, the following principles were frequently confirmed during weekly power-user group meetings:

1. Minimization of duplication.

2. Design for end-users by end-users.

3. Focus on the importance of dataflow.

4. Minimization of changes in job procedures.

5. Reuse of past resources.

Power-user group working members could easily fix document layouts according to their job procedures or interactions because they daily worked on it in their own sections as experts. Another merit of creating document layouts was cooperation. Individual power-users initially started on demand in their own sections, but soon realized the necessity of meeting with those in other sections to create documents organically. Besides group work, small-scale meetings also came about naturally for related power-users to clarify present job procedures and dataflow. When the need for system review was identified, the problems at hand were taken as subjects for discussion in regular group work.

These operations were performed during the introduction of the EMR system. Though every power-user also played a great role in setting up this system, they carried heavy responsibilities and their stress for workload became hard.

2.2. Interface with the EMR System

The EMR system publishes commands for exclusive usage of FileMaker files. To transfer data from this system, our vendor originally presented protocols to send packet CSV files outlining each patient's basic profile to individual client terminals. Using these files, FileMaker Pro could create records for individual patients. The vendor also supported the creation of documents with additional original functions using the FileMaker Pro system.

In this method, patient data sources were limited and there was less potential for future expansion of the interface between FileMaker Pro and the EMR system. Accordingly, we asked the vendor to come up with a more flexible and expansive method. Subsequently, FileMaker Pro Ver. 4 was given the capacity to connect to SQL data sources through SQL queries. The recent FileMaker Pro Ver. 9 is also able to create secure two-way connections to external SQL data sources (ESS) through FileMaker Pro tables without the need for users to write SQL queries or have SQL programming skills. Using this protocol, the support vendor was able to provide various SQL tables according to individual customer requirements in the same way, and customers (end-users) can easily connect SQL data tables directly. This was a big step for end-users who used only FileMaker Pro without SQL skills.

However, these developments open up the risk of end-user error when accessing SQL data tables directly. When these data are directly sorted or rewritten, the transaction performance may cause serious latency for transaction because the system was designed with two-way connection in real time. Considering the purpose of our system (document-oriented, computing-based operation), quotation from various patients' data tables was sufficient to make patient documents. For this reason, the system data were restricted to one-way flow (from the EMR system to the FileMaker Pro system). These connected ODBC data were restored to FileMaker Pro files as outlined below at the timing of Front-end file connection to ODBC data resources.

2.3. FileMaker Pro File Creation

Integrated FileMaker Pro file creation for the document-oriented, computing-based system

File creation is implemented as follows:

1. Front-end files.
2. Patient files.
3. Bed status files.
4. Common patient resource files.
5. Document creation files.
6. Educational files.

The role of each file type is outlined below.

2.3.1. Front-End Files

The main file for front-end operation was constructed as a log-in file for the FileMaker Pro system (except for a number of specific tasks) to fulfill order-entry system requirements or allow the use of educational files. Before logging into the FileMaker Pro system, users have to select a specific patient using the "Entry" or "Bed board" files of the EMR system by taking the patient's latest data as a CSV file from it. In line with these data, a new log-in file record is created for the start of any task on the FileMaker Pro system. Once this file is created, patient files and common patient resource files are requested to allow access to the most up-to-date detailed patient data from the EMR system using ESS. If the same user starts to use another log-in file record before closing the current patient's session on the same terminal, the old record is closed, a new record for the other patient is created, and the same procedure is followed to obtain the most up-to-date patient data from the EMR system. Even after another patient is selected using an "Entry" or "Bed board" file in the EMR system before closing this log-in file record (*i.e.*, the user is still working with the latest patient log-in file record, and CSV data from the EMR system are rewritten for another patient, this log-in file acts to renew the CSV data for latest patient to avoid erroneous operation).

Another front-end file type was constructed to act as master files with the roles of maintaining coherence between the master files of the FileMaker Pro system and those of the EMR system and restricting direct end-user access to SQL tables. In particular, employee data tend to change frequently in contrast to invariable data such as those specifying the department or floor. To avoid complicated maintenance in the FileMaker Pro system, an employee master file is utilized to renew employee data from the EMR system using ESS. This file is used when log-in file records, patient files and common patient resource files are created for synchronization to the EMR system.

2.3.2. Patient Files

Although the EMR system managed a large number of patient profiles, there was still a significant lack of patient profiles for document creation. The purpose of both patient files and common patient resource files was to allow the transfer of detailed patient profiles from the EMR system to the FileMaker Pro system and enable data input by users. Front-end files play an important role in reducing the burden of data transfer. Every log-in file record is opened with these files to collect patient profiles from the EMR system, and is collated with the original data for renewal. When the end-user performs any task, these files ensure transfer of the most up-to-date patient profiles to the operation files. The difference between patient files and common patient resource files is whether the information they contain may have multiple versions or not. Patient files handle items such as social status, disability insurance, nursing care insurance, allergy history, family tree and lifestyle information. These data tend to change infrequently, and usually require only one-time input for document creation. On the other hand, common patient resource files handle variable data such as height, weight, state of transfer and name of medical condition. These data may have multiple entries, and require historical context for document creation.

2.3.3. Bed Status Files

These files perform three roles for tasks relating to inpatient hospitalization. One role is to create a relationship between necessary inpatient documents and unique hospitalizations. Another is to share the details of patient sub-orders that are not supported by the EMR system especially for nursing staff. The final role is to act as a patient interface for hospitalization to enable storage of patient status assessment (stored in patient files) as raw materials for document creation.

For the first role, the unique record number of the file is sent over to each record of every document file in the request. In this process, all documents are classified for each hospitalization.

In Japan, most medical expenses are covered by national health insurance. Accordingly, each period of hospitalization involves many indispensable documents (regarding contracts, evaluations, reports, and so on) for billing to the national health insurance organization. To ensure accurate management, all documents relating to inpatient treatment and care are assigned a unique number for every hospitalization. Sometimes, doctors must prepare these documents accurately themselves, as support from medical clerks or assistants has become more narrowly permitted in recent years. For this reason, these files are intentionally not synchronized from the bed control files of the EMR system.

The second role is to prepare the information view for niche orders supplied by EMR system, such as augmentations with requirements in various situations or special department orders. Although the basic core system gives details about medication orders, injection orders and care processes on daily charts, it indicates busy view to display these precise information on a daily doctor's plan on the screen.

One of the advantages of a paper-oriented system is that it allows such quick inspection. Accordingly, FileMaker Pro files for such orders were designed with a layout similar to that of the original order sheet. This similarity is considered because it would reduce the burden on doctors and nursing staff more than a different layout would. Unfortunately, the need to keep these orders on the same page as seen in manual operation was not observed. One reason for this was that such a working style requires arbitrary judgment to start a new page in a paper-based system, and another was the deep-strata nature of such a layout within the system (in the new version, this problem is addressed).

The final role relates to patient assessments originally included in paper documents upon admission by nursing staff. For such operation, staff originally had to retype the same heading on other documents for scoring. In the FileMaker Pro system, this scoring step is performed automatically and the calculated data are reflected in other document file records to avoid the need for retyping. To ensure a feeling of similarity to the procedure of the paper-based system, the patient profile fields in patient files and common patient resource files are relationally oriented in the same layout.

2.3.4. Common Patient Resource Files

These files supply multiple data (*i.e.*, data that may have different entries, such as height, weight, state of transportation and past operation records) for patient document creation. They allow the transfer of data upon demand from document creation files. To ensure updating of these files, a startup script is included to obtain the latest data from the EMR system when the front-end file is opened.

2.3.5. Document Creation Files

These files show true worth of end user computing in the FileMaker Pro system. The four file types outlined above store information on operation status and patient profiles for document preparation. Although their maintenance and creation are restricted to users with administrator privileges in the interests of system stability and security, they can also be opened by power-users for table, field, layout and script creation. Upon request from a power-user, an administrator can allow linkage between document creation files and three other file types, patient files, bed status files and common patient resource files. All maintenance rights relating to document creation files belong to the power-user, and if the user in charge changes, the new user can take over this maintenance easily because the basic structure of these document creation files is the same as that of the vendor's model for the core electronic paper chart system.

There are two methods for approving documents made by the FileMaker Pro system. In one, they are approved and kept in PDF format directly on the EMR server, and in the other they are printed in paper form with a QR code including the document title, the date of printing, data on the handling terminal and staff member, the patient's basic information and other details. Patients or staff members can sign or check boxes, words or sentences on these printed versions according to their interaction. After the relevant marks and notes are made, the documents are scanned and approved as PDF files according to their QR codes in the EMR system, and officially become part of the system once this approval is secured. Scanning is performed in individual wards or scanning centers for outpatient documents. Information on the scanning date, time, terminal and staff member is kept as background data in the electronic chart system.

2.3.6. Educational Files

These files are prepared for user education. One type is an incident/accident report file, and the other is an e-learning file for newcomer training. When a user logs into the EMR system before patient selection, the system transfers CSV data including only the user code and the terminal code. Using this data, these files can be started before patient identification and can identify the personal code and terminal code after log-in.

The files are related to the construction of log-in tables, supervision tables and working tables. The first type of table works as a window for observation of all users and manages permitted layouts according to security policy. The second type lists each individual log-in record and collects results from working tables.

3. RESULT AND DISCUSSION (ADVANTAGES AND DISADVANTAGES)

The unified layout given by providing front-end files above all document files at the beginning of tasks brings a number of advantages. The first is the generation of a trigger to gather the latest patient information, which may change at any time. In consideration of server loads and terminal usage, it is not practical to constantly obtain up-to-date synchronized information at all times; this trigger works on demand when the user needs to be presented with the latest data on the screen. The reduced load that this method creates was preferable for small scale non powerful database system such as FileMaker server system. Secondly, checking of user behavior can be performed to some degree from the log file. Although there are not yet enough log functions, this is comparatively helpful for monitoring in the event of abnormalities.

Another characteristic of this system is facilitation using ESS, which is helpful for the development of applications in our hospital. ESS makes such development easier while reducing the number of steps required on the vender side. Possible problems in terms of running speed and security when using ESS with FileMaker have been pointed out. For the former problem, the role of FileMaker was specialized as one of document creation and rules were set with assumed unidirectional information flow from the server to FileMaker, with no data written directly to the server side. This rule is also effective for the latter problem. However, the feeling of unification in operability may be impaired because the user cannot perform data entry into the EMR system through FileMaker fields.

Patient data sources reconstructed by FileMaker are used flexibly within the FileMaker system. For availability using the data sources in each document, integration and adjustment were required, and the EUC strategy was valid for rapid negotiation on such tasks between each job section because individual power-users had high levels of skill regarding their own specific areas and recognized the necessity of unified data sources and data flow process. Power-users therefore developed applications for many duties according to a variety of job types using FileMaker directly. From this benefit, even if the duties were changed by the national health insurance organization, documents for their requirement could be arranged by the EUC strategy quickly and exactly. After the introduction of this system, negotiation between power-users was re-examined in regard to site needs or job alternation as with the PDCA cycle approach [2].

However, differences in the levels of various applications and variations in operating environments seem to have given rise to a number of problems. In addition, there have also been issues with application maintenance when the person in charge resigns.

The subsystem of the electronic chart system created by FileMaker was made with a directionality whereby changes from the paper-based system workflow as a result of the addition of new duties would be minimized as much as possible, and information already input could be reused wherever feasible. The advantage of this system was the similar layouts for end users on filling up these documents with the past paper-based system. End users suffered less from disorientation and misunderstanding.

This is still only the beginning of the fusion of paper-based and electronic systems. Although information on paper – an important medium that has been used for several thousand years – can now be represented electronically in various fields, it does not need to be wholly eliminated from our duties. Our fusion system provides solutions in one direction, but it should also be asked whether we can also envisage goals in other directions. Even if we do not see them at present, our answer must be, “Yes, we can”.

CONFLICT OF INTEREST

None declared.

ACKNOWLEDGEMENTS

This system was presented at the 29th Joint Conference on Medical Informatics 2009 in Japan. The author is grateful to the researchers present at these conferences for their comments. The author is also appreciative to the engineers of Ryobi Systems for advice at San-in Rosai Hospital.

REFERENCES

[1] Brancheau C, Brown V. The Management of End-User Computing: Status and Direction. ACM Computing Surveys 1993; 25(4): 437-482.

[2] Letort NR, Boudreaux J. Incorporation of continuous quality improvement in a hospital dietary department's quality management program. J Am Diet Assoc 1994; 94(12): 1404-8.

CHAPTER 5

Hospital Information System at Osaka National Hospital: Input/Output and Reference System Using FileMaker

Atsuhiko Okagaki*

Osaka National Hospital, 2-1-14 Hoenzaka, Chuo-Ku, Osaka, Japan

Abstract: Electronic Medical Record System (EMR) has some weakness in their usability. The weakness is due to adopting "Waterfall" method to every part of the system. To get rid of those problems, our hospital uses FileMaker Pro to input/output Electronic Medical Record. In our system, all clinical data of a patient will be spread out on FileMaker when one would like to open a record. Then, added information when saving the record will be transferred to basic system. The input-output layouts can be modified easily as user need, and several functions can be introduced very easily. Our system is so flexible that we can easily customize all the layouts as requested by any department of a large-scale general hospital and those of clinical supporting system. In addition to the flexibility of the interface layer, another benefit of our system is that FileMaker layer can be used as the viewer of multi-vender system.

Keywords: Electronic medical record, FileMaker Pro, Usability, Flexibility, Interface, Agile, End user computing, Reference system, User-made, Clinical supporting system, J-SUMMITS.

1. HISTORY AND CURRENT CONDITION OF HOSPITAL INFORMATION SYSTEM

Back to 80's, general hospitals started to use computer to support hospital operations. At the time, hospitals only had medical account's calculation system. Although, the system had expanded around in the year 1995. Now in the new system, they use computer to input prescription data including oral medicine and injection drug instead of handwriting. The data goes to pharmaceutical department and medical accountant, and input test item information goes to blood-drawing room so they can collect blood as soon as possible. After that, doctor can see the results in doctor's office. Then the data goes to medical accountant.

***Address correspondence to Atsuhiko Okagaki:** Department of Gynecology, Osaka National Hospital, Japan; E-mail: okagaki3@onh.go.jp

Shunji Wakamiya, Kazunobu Yamauchi and Hiroyuki Yoshihara (Eds)

This new system was improved again in 1999 at Shimane Prefectural Central Hospital. Since inputting those data to computer and writing on medical record is double work, they started to use Electronic Medical Record using the computer. This was the first Electronic Medical Record in Japan. People were worried about how smooth medical care can go using Electronic Medical Record. The reason is that Electronic Medical Record does not have useful function unlike old one. Previous medical records, especially in first visit, were divided into major complaint, clinical history, anamnesis, family history, physical findings, examination findings, evaluation, therapeutic plan and so on. Moreover, they had tags or made with different colors of paper so that surgical records, examination records, and summaries can be easily found.

Electronic Medical Records had a search system that one could use by typing sentence or keywords. Still specific information or merged information of specific items could not be viewed. In other words, Electronic Medical Records were not for everyday examinations because they were not built for extracting information required. This problem was not solved until after 10 years. As a result, it was so difficult to know patients' history that we needed.

That is, it is easy to search data of testing or accounting, but it is difficult to analyze free text and extract specific data. In addition, hospital operation is very complicated in many departments. Actually, the operation was not going smoothly with paper-based records. Everyone was hoping computerized systems would improve the operation, but it was not so easy. Useful structure was not built yet because programming vender could not analyze operation at hospital.

Therefore, Electronic Medical Records have many problems. Especially doctors are opposing to it because Electronic Medical Records are tricky to use compared to paper-basis. You might think that is because many doctors are not very good at typing, but actually they are familiar with computers. Besides, it usually is faster and easier to type than writing on paper. Not only typing, but the problem is the difficulty in knowing history, taking time to input prescription and test in ordering, and hardness of correcting.

Now, let us go through what it was like with paper records. As I mentioned earlier, mostly they were divided into small items with the first visit (Figs. **1**, **2**).

In cases with after second visit and hospitalization, there are drawn lines and doctors fill out freely. In those cases, it is normal to have nothing on it or maybe a little note. It usually is hard to read for someone else and that is a problem when the data is paper-based. One of the purposes of introducing Electronic Medical Records is enabling to provide better healthcare as a team by letting doctors fill out records in cases of hospitalization and after second visit. As I went through old paper records, they are awful （Figs. **3**, **4**） and it is hard to believe that it worked in old times.

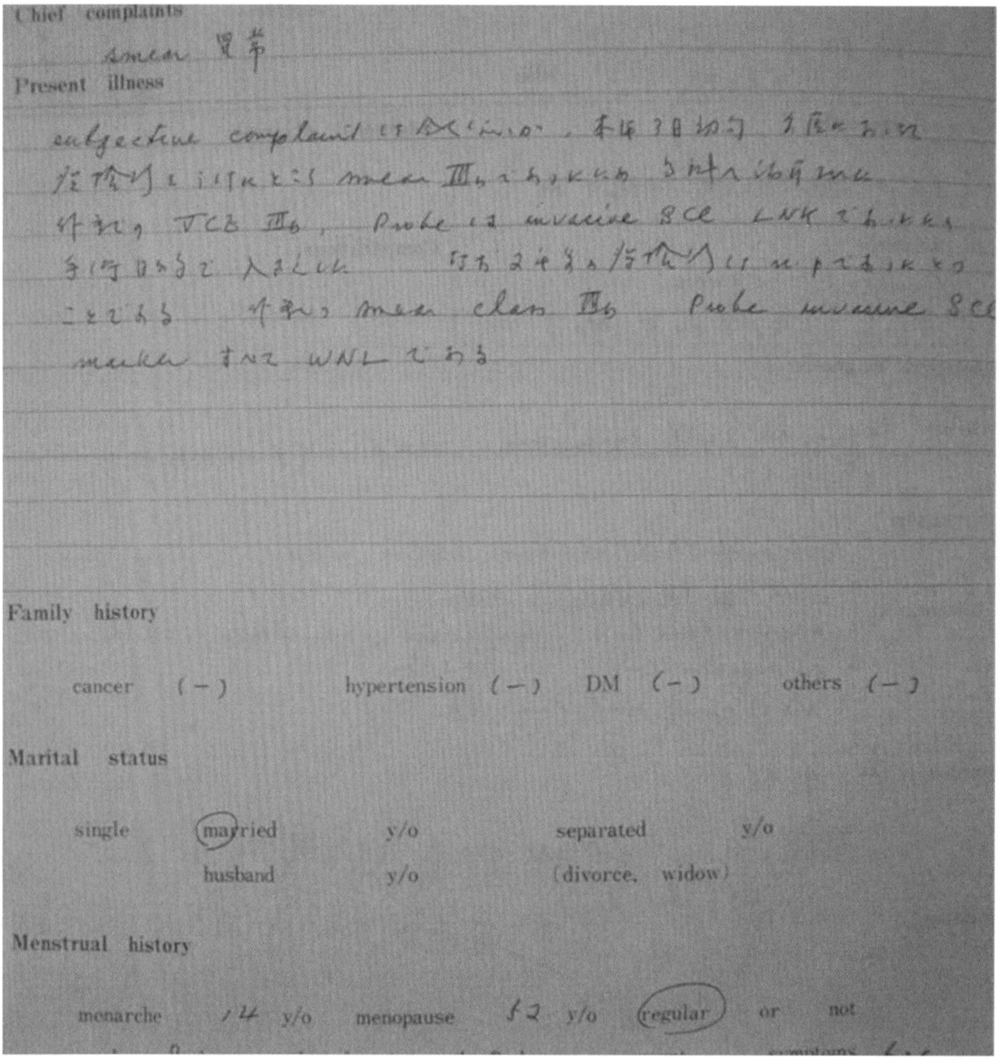

Chief complaints

Present illness

subjective complaint

Family history

cancer (−) hypertension (−) DM (−) others (−)

Marital status

single married y/o separated y/o

husband y/o (divorce, widow)

Menstrual history

menarche 14 y/o menopause 52 y/o regular or not

Figure 1: “Paper” medical record for New Patient; by interview.

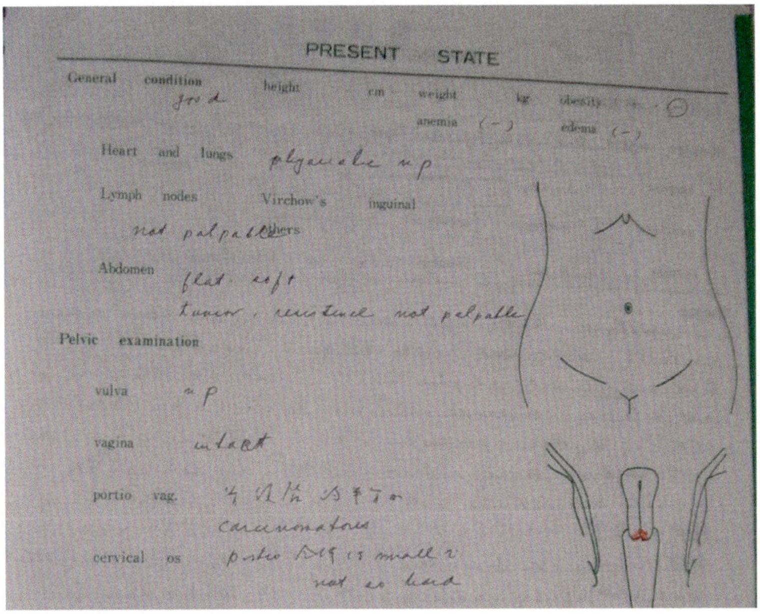

PRESENT STATE

General condition good height cm weight kg obesity
anemia (−) edema (−)

Heart and lungs np

Lymph nodes Virchow's inguinal
not palpable others

Abdomen flat soft
tumor, resistence not palpable

Pelvic examination

vulva np

vagina intact

portio vag.

carcinomatous

cervical os

not so hard

Figure 2: "Paper" medical record for New Patient; Physical examination.

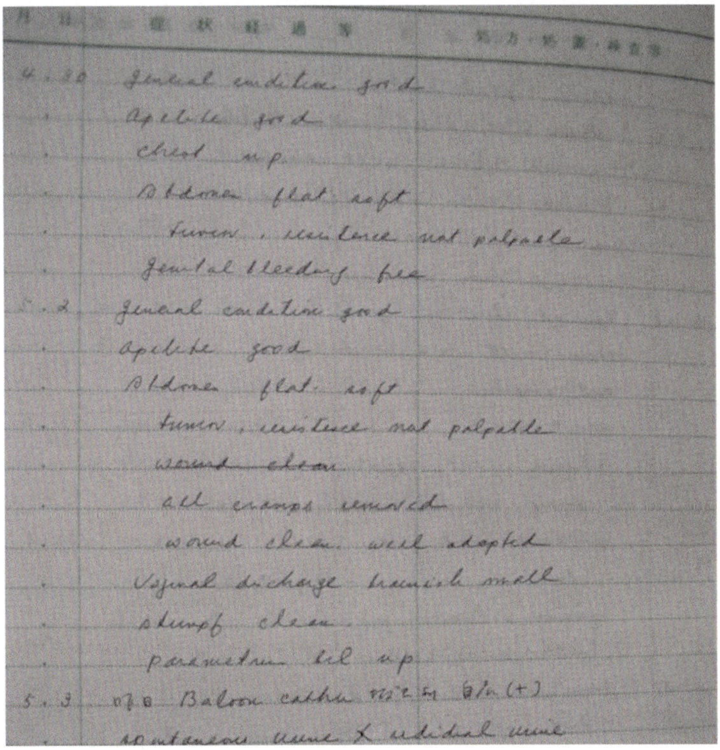

4.20 general condition good
apetite good
chest np
Abdomen flat soft
tumor, resistence not palpable
genital bleeding free
5.2 general condition good
apetite good
Abdomen flat soft
tumor, resistence not palpable
wound clean
All cramps removed
wound clean well adapted
Vaginal discharge brownish small
stumpf clean
parametrium bil np
5.3 Baloon catheter (+)
spontaneous urine residual urine

Figure 3: Well described "Paper" medical redord.

Thus, we can figure out how Electronic Medical Records should be. They should have some required items in writing, and should be sorted out with general clinical records, surgery, testing and summary to make it easy to refer, while it has to be simple to understand the progress. You can only see limited information on your screen at once. Hence, you should be able to switch window to get more information and at the same time, user should not be confused. However, there is no such Electronic Medical Record product.

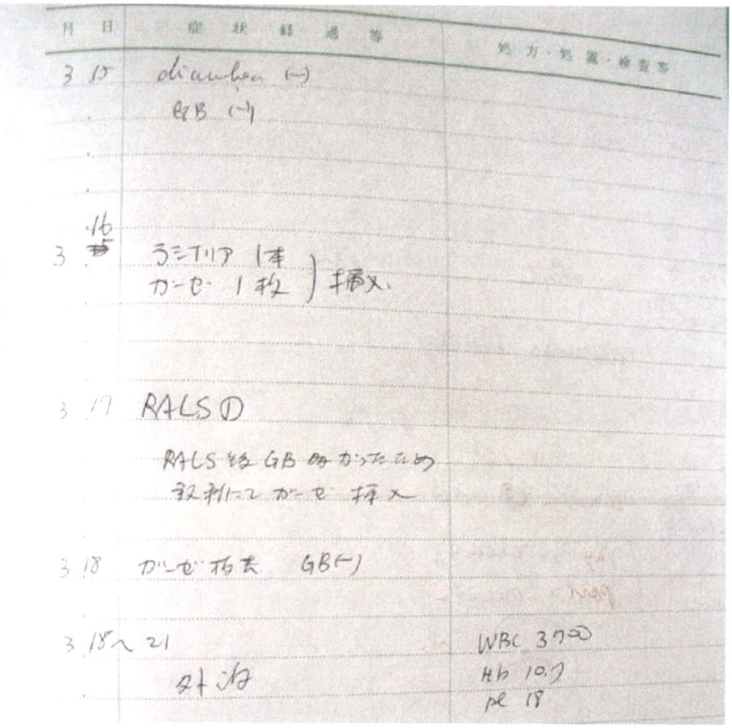

Figure 4: Poorly described "Paper" medical record.

2. LATER USE SYSTEM

Major reason to introduce Hospital Information System is that we can analyze several things using stored data on the system. In reality, we have problems in using information well. In Hospital Information System, databases are separated into two, for reference and for operation. Reference database is called reference system or DWH (Data Warehouse). The medical accounting system data is the best to be used in Hospital Information System. For example, it is easy to get data of hospital income sorted by insurance type, ages and residence. Although, it is not easy with expenses. In case of searching if there is summary of a discharged patient or not, it is not possible to do with searching system vender constructed. We need another system for that. In case of creating a list of patients with cancer, we need to compare their general disease name, the DPC (Diagnosis Procedure Combination), pathological examination, and history of anticancer drug use. If we want to search something complicated like this, it is impossible to do it with default system. Moreover, it may be expensive and time-consuming. These needs are common in hospital operation, but there's no reference system provided by major vendors that can cross search several information.

Now let us talk about using information afterward with paper-base records. We used special database called "ledger" in hospital operation for matters that need statistical work and comparative discussion. In actual situation, many hospitals operate because there are no computerized ledgers in Hospital Information System. However, it is natural to try to use computer to create a ledger since there already is a system with network. If the database works stand-alone, we need double work to input patients' general information like ID (Identification number) and name on the ledger and Hospital Information System. Due to this, we should transfer patients' information from Hospital Information System, match the data and then it will be labor-saving and avoidance of inputting error. This is an approach of user-made-system and if data-transferring system works properly, it means we are almost there to make great improvement.

Almost all operation data are stored in Hospital Information System. In many cases, data are decentral on different database or everything is on the same database. In such system, only way to link them is to use patient ID, date created, or identity number on Electronic Medical Record of parent document that issued the data. To combine these information and get useful data, you need to know both database structure and clinical practice.

3. ISSUES WITH DEVELOPMENT METHOD OF VENDERS

Generally, there are two methods of program development, waterfall method and agile method (Fig. **5**). In waterfall method, the progress is seen like a waterfall going downwards strictly following phases as planned. The phases are Requirements Specification, Analysis, Design, Construction, implementation and Testing. In principle, there's no stepping back. This method is suitable for large-scale system development, which has clear requirements specification with no changes during development. This method origins in an article "Managing the Development of Large Software Systems" written by Winston W. Royce in 1970 [1]. In this article, he included feedback between each process. Later on, because feedback itself will be an obstacle to develop by deadline efficiently, no feedback with this method became popular. Although, this method ended up with many project failures. Meanwhile, Rational Unified Process was suggested which is generally called "Agile Method" means almost the same. This quick, light and adoptive recursion development method (Fig. **6**) was discussed by developers in 2001, and they published "Agile Manifesto" [2].

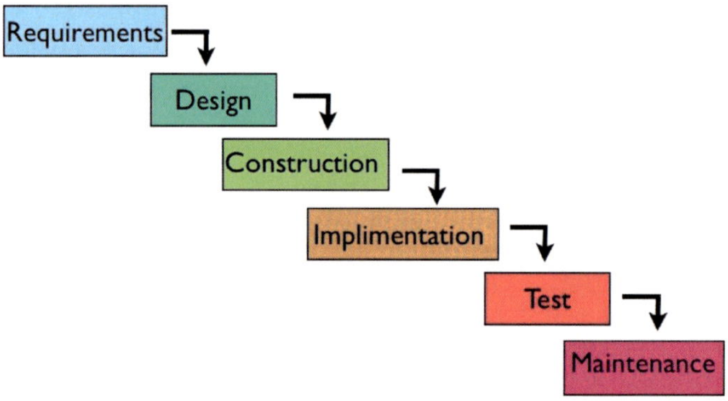

Figure 5: Waterfall Development.

Figure 6: Agile Development.

When you look at Hospital Information System in several hospitals, you can see the characteristics of product developed with waterfall method. More specifically, these systems were developed by deadline with functions on requested specifications, but it is tricky to use when it comes to each department. In other words, on-site operation is not analyzed properly. For example, you have to click 10 times for an action, which should be done with 1 click, or you have to type the same words many times. This can happen because it is so difficult to describe on-site operations on a document that it already has a problem in the phase of Requirements Specification. I think it is pretty impossible to describe the operations on a document to begin with. In these situations, understanding operation details, creating test application, using on-site and then modifying it on and on will develop an ideal system. This is called agile method.

Typically, budget and deadline are tight in Japan. So developing Hospital Information System is done with waterfall method, and then department system will be added by using waterfall method taking in agile method only if they can afford extra expenses. Therefore, many Hospital Information Systems show adverse effects of waterfall method. Disadvantages of Electronic Medical Record I mentioned earlier are just a part of problems in Hospital Information System. Many issues are unsolved because developing method is not right (Fig. **7**).

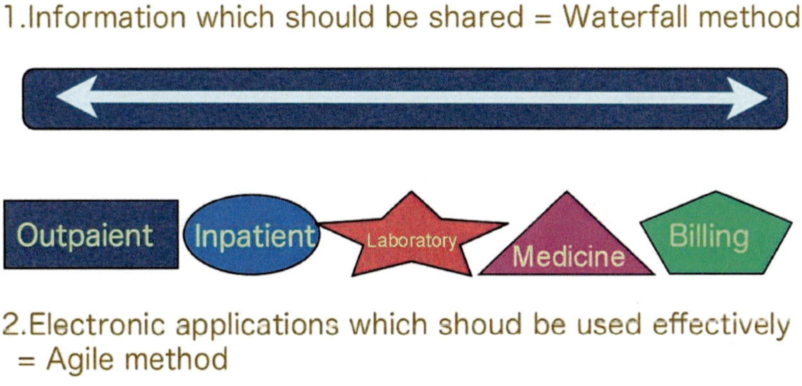

Figure 7: Local applications should be constructed by Agile method, whereas basic database may be constructed by waterfall method.

Electronic Medical Record was first introduced to Japan in 1999. Basically, a system in a hospital will be replaced in 5 to 6 years. Hospital Information System developed by major vendors will be third generation in 2010. The first generation could be an adequate help because it was developed with waterfall method. Now, they already have got feedbacks for 3 generations of product. So improvement on Hospital Information System is slowly paying off. However, even whole products of manufacturers are improved; hospitals replace the system in few years. That means specially improved part for a hospital with agile method will be reset in many cases. Especially when a hospital change vender, they may have to develop the system from scratch.

When I think about these matters, it is a very good idea to create user interface as a stand-alone application with agile method, and transfer it when the basic system is changed so that improved part can be taken over.

There is a third method, which is neither waterfall nor agile, called End User Computing (EUC). Users develop a system in this method. It is hard and takes time to develop and operate system that works in actual operation on-site, if you leave everything to outside contractors or information system department. So operating department leads developing process, but usually hospital administrators do not accept as an official duty.

The system developed with waterfall does not work smoothly in operation, and it is a big trouble for the staffs on-site. Vendors do not schedule developing in agile method when introducing a system. Hospitals with many extra budgets after introducing can make it work somehow, but hospitals without it have to go with that or use EUC I mentioned to create department system. Staffs must create the system outside of their work because operations do not go smoothly. In on-site operation, it has a lot of advantages more than make up for it. For hospital administrators, this means less reliability and more worries about information leak because the system is made on their own, not officially. This is how End User Computing was born in Japanese hospitals. There are many problems like this with EUC, but it is high quality because someone creates it with much knowledge about operation. So this way works perfectly in the point of getting better operation. Recently, many hospitals officially promote this method from security standpoint. Japan EUC Institute and J-SUMMITS [3] who publish this book, are a group of people who assent this movement.

4. PLACING FILEMAKER Pro ON VENDER's ELECTRONIC MEDICAL RECORD INTERFACE LAYER

As I stated earlier, existing Electronic Medical Record has problems with operating and browsing. Although, it is almost impossible to improve vender's Electronic Medical Record and it will cost a lot if you try to improve inadequately. To get rid of those problems, our hospital uses FileMaker Pro to input/output Electronic Medical Record [4]. In our system, all clinical data of a patient will be spread out on FileMaker when you open a record. Then added information while saving the record will be transferred to basic system (Fig. **8**). Out attempt is to fit EUC method in developing schedule of Hospital Information System from the beginning. On the whole we use waterfall method, but we use EUC method for basic structure of records and agile method for the part to develop with vender in cooperation. The base system is Fujitsu's EG-Main EX Ver.6, and FileMaker Pro version 8 and 9 for several reasons. Patient's data from mission-critical system will be transferred to FileMaker Pro as local database on a terminal and be spread out and then while records input or saved will be sent to mission-critical system in our structure. Basic structure of data transferring between mission-critical system and interface layer is standardized in all branch and differences in record form and action between each branch will be processed on interface layer.

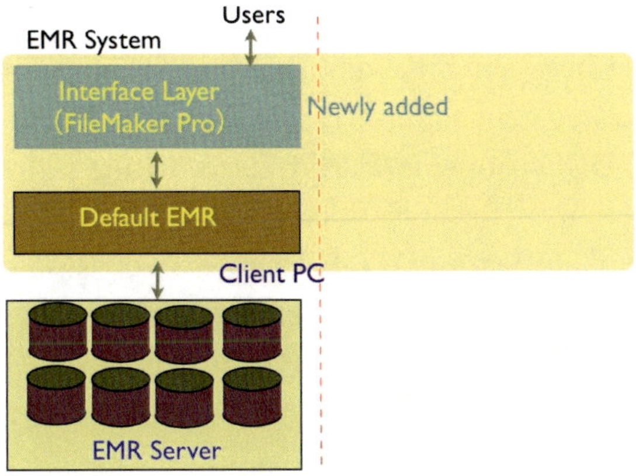

Figure 8: Structure of EMR of Osaka National Hospital.

All orders read out of Electronic Medical Records will be synchronized between FileMaker and mission-critical system at all times. In our system, with cooperation of mission-critical system and interface layer, for example, it is possible to build interface layer with other than FileMaker like Excel, Word, or Access. We can customize interface part flexibly without changing the record itself.

Our system solved the problem by improving the maintenance contract depending on clinical staff's needs on interface made with FileMaker Pro, which is a different application from the record itself. We can use FileMaker Pro to make changes, so that it will make the system flexible and stable.

Moreover, we introduced reference system using FileMaker Pro server and transfer data from Electronic Medical Record server. It makes possible for us to browse on the same layout of input. In addition to general clinical record layout, we installed modality of input with ledger style, called Clincal Support System in which we can input like clinical records so that staff can display lists, search, and statistical process on reference system.

We started using this system at obstetrics department, internal medicine department, and circulatory in April 2000. In April 2006, all departments started using the system.

5. STRUCTURE OF DATA TRANSFERRING

For transferring data between Electronic Medical Records on each terminal and FileMaker Pro, we tested connection with HL7, CSV (Comma Separated Values) -cooperation, and ODBC-cooperation and more. In the point of throughput, we chose CSV-cooperation. After creating various CSV files including records, testing data, disease name, and order information on mission-critical system while Electronic Medical Record is open; the control goes to FileMaker Pro and load data in series. After the record is input, the data will be saved by opposite action. Order information will be sent to mission-critical system arbitrarily while Electronic Medical Record is in use but there is a problem. It will take time to create and read CSV files. After 600 records, we have a major problem that takes time to create CSV files. We are trying to make it work drastically. It is palliative way, but we narrow down data to transfer to shorten starting time.

6. FILEMAKER Pro REFERENCE SYSTEM

As I mentioned earlier, in Hospital Information System, databases are separated into two, for reference and for operation. Reference database is called reference system or DWH. Usually, the data contents are almost all information on Hospital Information System, but as I previously mentioned, it only can do simple search and it takes time to search. To solve this problem, we decided to add reference system to the system using FileMaker Pro server. First, the record information input on FileMaker Pro will be transferred to reference system server while saving on mission-critical system. At the same time, the data will be sent to FileMaker Pro server *via* CSV file (Fig. **9**). Thus, data on FileMaker pro are converted to mission-critical system format, saved on mission-critical system server, and then restored to original format on FileMaker Pro server.

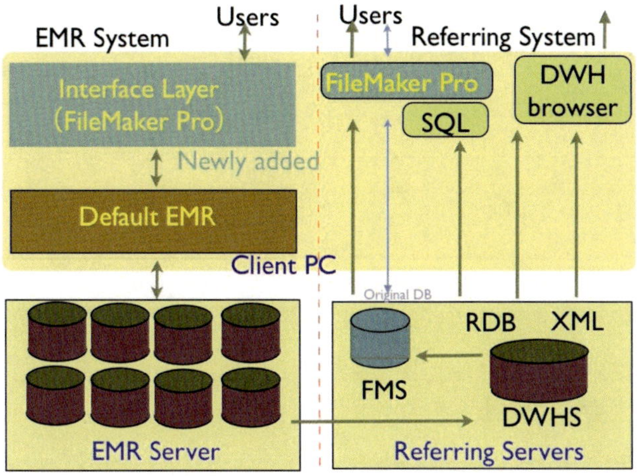

Figure 9: Structure of EMR and Referring system of Osaka National Hospital.

Therefore, we have XML (Extensible Markup Language) reference system (a.k.a. downtime record) that comes with vender's Electronic Medical Record, RDB (Relational Database) reference system (DWH reference system), and reference system with FileMaker Pro server. Now we are able to cross-search, cross-browse in the same layout with input layout.

As stated above, ledgers called Clinical Supporting System, in which we can input just as Electronic Medical Record, can be used to list information *via* FileMaker Pro server. In this system, we can add and change the layout for listings and we can do advanced search by using script. This strongly shows advantages of building reference system using FileMaker Pro. Hence, using FileMaker Pro for reference system will make it possible for us to have special application that needs advanced search with the least work and time. You can see the list of ledgers made with FileMaker Pro in Table **1**, and list of searching system combined with existing data in Table **2**.

Table 1: Clinical supporting system

Bedsore Record;
Cancer treatment support team
Medical Social Worker
Palliative for psychologists
Hospital cancer registration of Japanese-Association of Cancer Registry
Surgical Site Infection Report
Surveillance of Multidrug-resistant –Organisms
Fall and knock-down Prevention
Stoma Care Record

Table 2: Searching system combined with existing data

Operation record of all Departments
Ledger of birth records
Ledger of the obstetric patients including baby due
Checking system for reply to the letter of introduction
Admission Summary

Now that data is clear, we can check which document we need, and check if required document has been written. With this system, we can check management additional charging, and check if patient is registered as a cancer patient who should be registered by crosschecking bedsore management ledger and medical data (Fig. **10**).

7. DEVELOPMENT

We developed FileMaker part at the same time with preparing for introducing Hospital Information System. The most important part is transferring system between FileMaker and vender's Hospital Information System. In addition to information on medical records, there's patient's profile, medical information, testing result and ordering issue to be transferred from FileMaker Pro. It is a very complicated system to do this smoothly. Mainly, vendor's expert engineer team did most work, but I designed special action on FileMaker Pro. The most difficult part is to make FileMaker Pro work in cooperation with mission-critical system smoothly when order is issued. Still, we did a very good job to solve problems. When we could be sure it will work stably, we decided base structure of FileMaker Pro and went on to developing FileMaker Pro part.

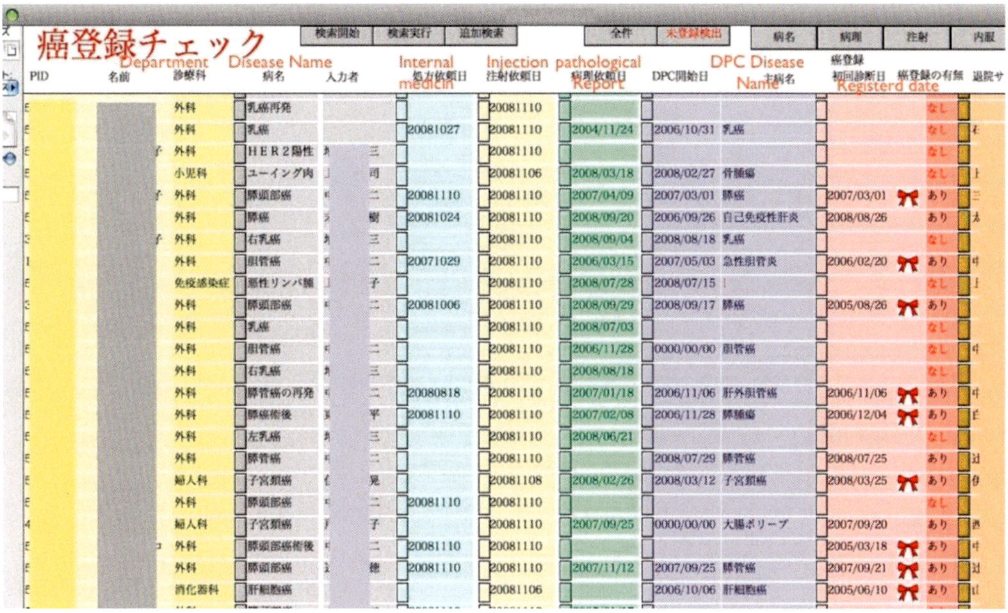

Figure 10: Cancer patient list for Hospital cancer registration picked up from various information.

We commissioned to someone who will actually use it design interface on developing FileMaker that each department uses. For interface of medical record, we chose representatives from each department to design interface. We created application on FileMaker Pro and tested under actual use, and improved again and again. This method is called agile software development and this is not the way normal Electronic Medical Record vendors use for developing. This could not be done without FileMaker Pro or something easy to handle and to improve. Programming of FileMaker Pro was done by Fujitsu system engineers and more than ten people programmed the system at the same time at one point. They had to learn about FileMaker because they did not know about it, and then development was done like a race. I am sure they had so much stress doing that. There are 14 departments in our hospital and in dentistry; the vendor-developed medical record was excellent. So they did not have to use FileMaker Pro. We developed FileMaker part for other departments and ledger system which I will discuss later. We did research on each department and installed items became about 650,000. It seems to be well managed with hierarchization (Fig. **11**).

◇	D	E	F	G	H	
1	ITEM_NAME	LAYOUT_NAME	ΛYOUT_NAM	EXTBCK_ITEI	BEFORE_STRING	AFTEF
19	眼圧アプラR Intraocular	再診	COMMON	Number15	 【眼圧アプラ】[RT=]	mmHg
20	眼圧アプラL pressure	再診	COMMON	Number18	[LT=]	mmHg
21	mX	再診	COMMON	Number2	 	μmX
22	SecX	再診	COMMON	Number3		secX
23	mWX	再診	COMMON	Number4		mWX
24	Shots	再診	COMMON	Number5		shots
25	BP1	再診	COMMON	Number54	[BP]	
26	BP2	再診	COMMON	Number55	/	mmg
27	(YAG)	再診	COMMON	Number6		shots (Y
28	Diode	再診	COMMON	Number7	【Diode】(	mm)
29	mX	再診	COMMON	Number8	 	μmX
30	SecX	再診	COMMON	Number9		secX
31	サマリ Summary	再診	COMMON	Text001	【サマリ】	
32	アレルギー allergy	再診	COMMON	Text002	【アレルギー】	
33	アレルギーフリー allergy free	再診	COMMON	Text003		
34	病名 Disease	再診	COMMON	Text004	【病名】	
35	散瞳 Mydriatic	再診	COMMON	Text013	【散瞳】	

Figure 11: Prepared fields for Opthalmology. Ordinary EMR for general usage.

There will be problems occurring when developing softwares like FileMaker Pro, which was made to be used privately, with many people at the same time. Someone else modifies at the same time or you cannot change according to what other person did. To prepare for that, we designed considering how operation goes before we started; like making basic part of transferring independent file and making sure that each group of operation has its own file, to be handy in developing. Since we are developing with many people, it is important to convey information and manage versions. We prepared a ledger to manage changed items as a groupware, made it impossible to make any change on one file at the same time, put comment on script every time we make a change, and built common rules like "Don't delete while the file is inactive". We built a system to distribute improved file in all hospitals, made rules to accept distributing, and built a system to record about distribution.

8. ADVANTAGES OF USER-MADE MEDICAL RECORD

User interface created with FileMaker Pro still has feelings of paper-base medical record. Record for first visit and surgery record look just like paper-based one. On the other hand, we made it possible to list in chronological order, which makes doctors understand patients' condition (Figs. **12-17**). This is so dynamic which can be done without computerizing. We tried to create display where you can get text and image information without switching window, while putting functions like list of surgery history and summary, and days after surgery or time point during pregnancy can be calculated and showed on records' main text field.We installed these functions individually for each department depending on their requests. Then we are able to provide applicable medical record for ophthalmology or obstetrics where they need special format. Furthermore, doctors can refer to other information on other departments' very own pages from their own terminals.

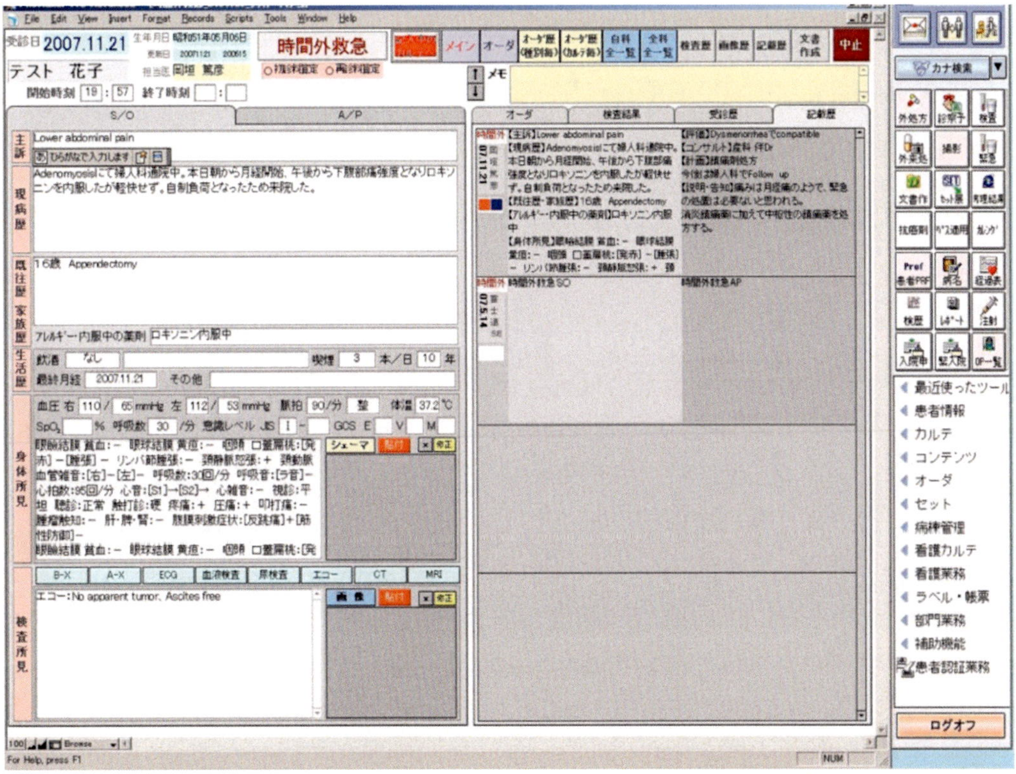

Figure 12: EMR for nighttime outpatient.

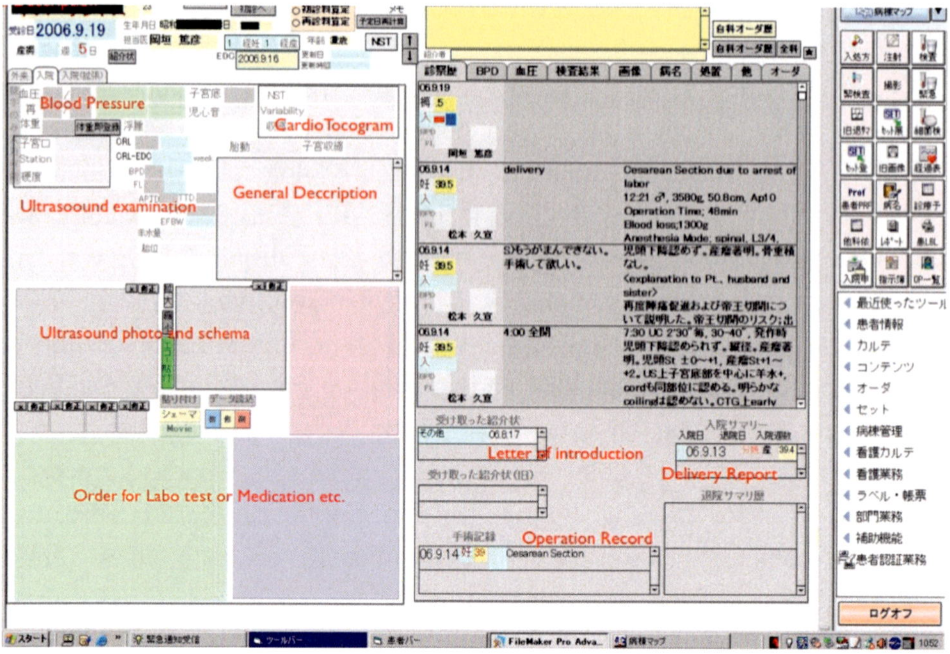

Figure 13: EMR for Obstetrics; Gestational week is calculated automatically.

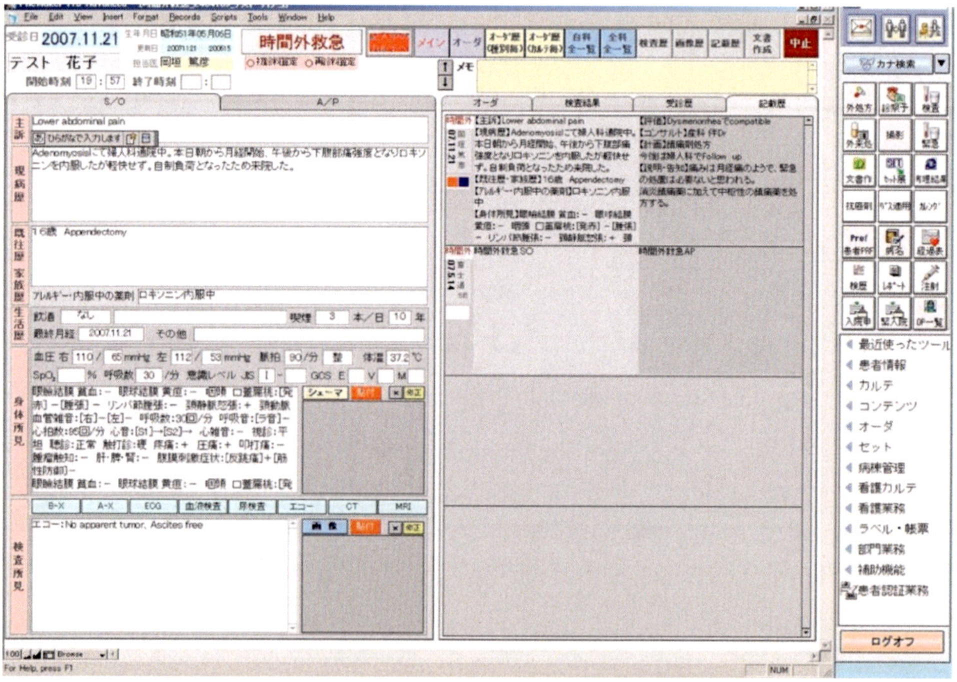

Figure 14: EMR for Opthalmology; Various sketches of anterior chamber are shown by time order. EMR for Opthalmology; Fundoscopy photos are shown by time order.

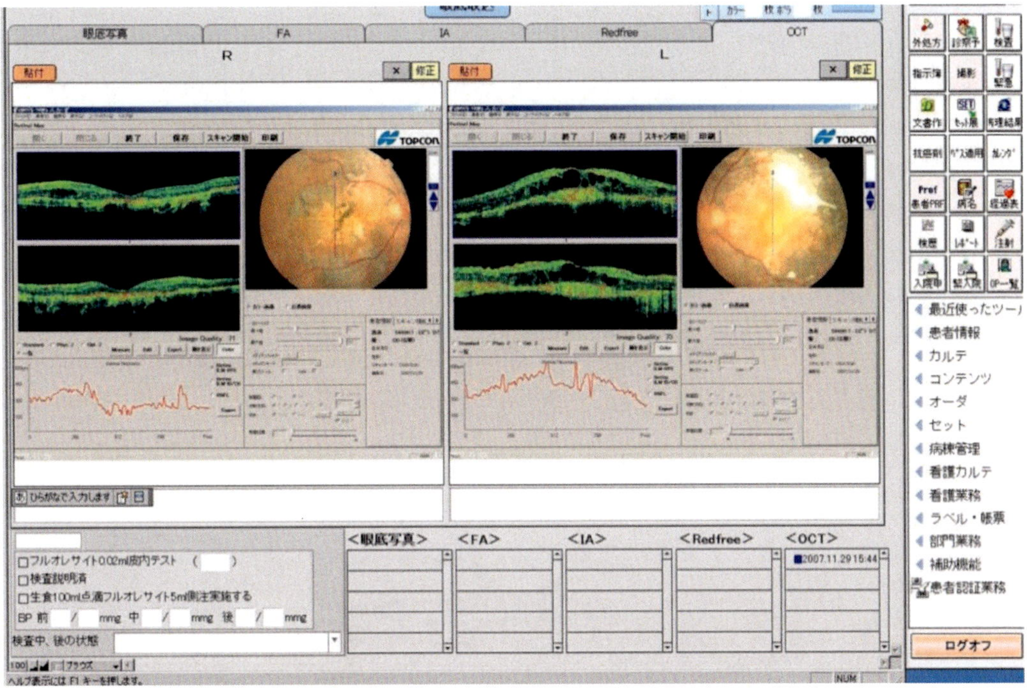

Figure 15: EMR for Opthalmology; Optical coherence tomography are shown.

FileMaker Pro is a really flexible software on graphical as well. So we were able to make the interface exactly the same look with user's idea sketch. I believe completed Electronic Medical Record became something ideal that users can think of, including how it behaves as it was programmed with FileMaker scripts. We still have a big problem with its speed. It sometimes runs slower than expected to load data and so on. We improved data transferring program and narrowed down data for faster behavior, and it is working with no problem in actual use. Still, it is major problem at this point.

9. OPERATING CONDITION

We found number of letters on medical records became 3 times as much as it used to be in paper-based records in obstetrics clinics (Fig. **16**).

When I look at hospitalized patients' paper-based records previously used, it's obvious that doctors started to record properly after Electronic Medical Record was introduced. On records of emergency room visit, especially residents use, detailed information on inquiry, examination, analyzing test results and upcoming policy. The average number of letters is 764 in 1 record. It is more than you can expect comparing to roll-paper Electric Medical records. Furthermore, 70% of principal items to input were filled out. I can say that we tried to fill out the form and it worked effectively. We are hoping doctors in training can pick up the habit to organize and store clinical data in their head by filling out the medical records.

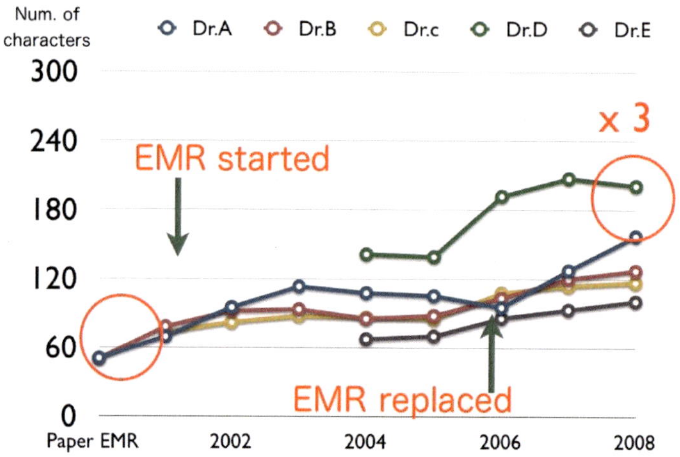

Figure 16: The change of number of characters to describe medical records in Obstetrics department.

10. POSTSCRIPT

Our system made Electronic Medical Record just like users want it to be and behave in FileMaker Pro part. Especially in describing, I am sure we made it as ideal as general users think of. Most doctors remember paper-based medical records as an ideal system. Generally, they added functions like finding data from testing or from past, but some other new ideas like checking if the records are following standard treatment plan can be found (Fig. **17**). The part built with FileMaker Pro, it is so easy to get used to that new doctors can operate them without training. I believe we could make "expected behavior" come true, that many doctors want. In ophthalmology, there's no idea of flipping paper-based record and records became something to use to compare with past data. This may show how medical records can go. In the future, I am sure there will be much convenient one when new interface ideas come up.

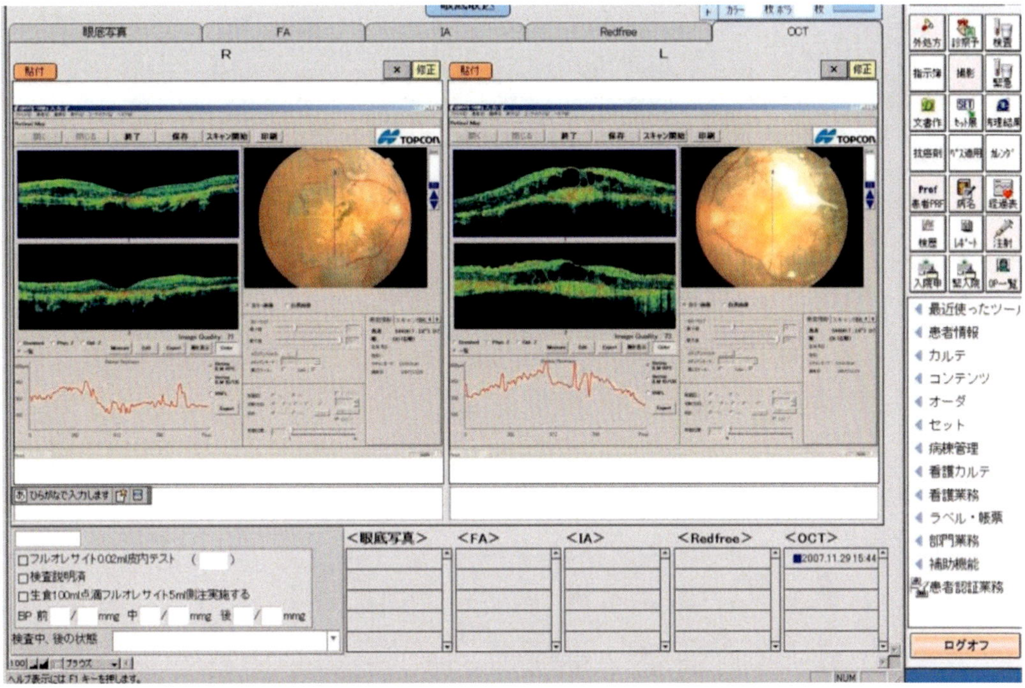

Figure 17: EMR for Surgery; Schedule for surveillance and actual examination are compared.

The system we built at our hospital could be something to fill up the time until major vendors develop very convenient Electronic Medical Record, but I hope this system can be a trigger to change current condition that medical efficiency goes down and clinical.

Finally, I wish to express my gratitude and thanks to Miss Shouko Matsushita and Miss Kumiko Sonoda who translated my original unpublished Japanese manuscript to good English.

CONFLICT OF INTEREST

None declared.

ACKNOWLEDGEMENT

None declared.

REFERENCES

[1] Winston W. Rovce, Managing the Development of Large Software Systems, Proceedings of IEEE Westcon, August 1970

[2] Agile Manifesto http://www.agileManifesto.org/ (2010.8.22)

[3] Japanese Society of User-Made Medical Systems http://www.j-summits.jp/index-1.html (2010.80.22)

[4] Okagaki, A,Koretsune, Y, Todo, R. Kusuoka, H., Complex Medical Engineering, 2007. CME 2007. IEEE/ICME, 23-27 May 2007, 287 – 290.

CHAPTER 6

Integration Between Hospital Information Systems and FileMaker Pro

Tetsu Nakamura*

Kakogawa East City Hospital, 797-295 Isshiki, Hiraoka, Kakogawa, Hyogo, Japan

Abstract: Although, computerization has been widely adopted in medical communities, it is often difficult for small-scale hospitals to make the large investments necessary to introduce electronic medical record systems, such as hospital information, radiology information, and picture archiving and communication systems (HIS, RIS, PACS, respectively). We have constructed medical information support systems with the commercial database software FileMaker Pro, which was also integrated with other hospital systems, such as PACS, ordering, and general account systems. Our FileMaker databases consist of master databases containing data regarding patient attributes, drug information, disease information, *etc.*, and operation databases consisting of administration, medical histories, examination schedules, imaging reports, operation plans, *etc.* FileMaker databases collect patient attributes from the general account system every 3 min. We developed an interface server for programs integration. The servers were connected with ODBC. After working with this cooperation program, we could reexamine operation of duties. Medical information support systems using FileMaker Pro are ideal for hospitals, because they can cooperate with other hospital systems or work as standalone systems. In a wide sense, this system can be defined as an electronic medical record, and it would be suitable for use in small-scale hospitals because of its low cost and ease of customization.

Keywords: Medical information supporting systems, digital divide, FileMaker Pro, small- scale hospital, electronic medical record systems, HIS, RIS, PACS, DICOM, ODBC, computerization, radiology, IHE, IHE-J, HL7.

1. INTRODUCTION

Computerization has been widely adopted in medical communities. However, it is often not easy for small-scale hospitals to invest the large amounts of resources required to introduce electronic medical record systems as well as hospital information systems (HIS), radiology information systems (RIS), and picture

***Address correspondence to Tetsu Nakamura:** Department of Radiology, Kakogawa East City Hopital, Japan; E-mail: t-nakamura@kakohp.jp

Shunji Wakamiya, Kazunobu Yamauchi and Hiroyuki Yoshihara (Eds)

archiving and communication systems (PACS). This will increase the digital division between large-scale hospitals and small-scale hospitals [1]. It is necessary that we consider cost performance related to hospital scale. First, we introduce our hospital, which is located between Kobe City and Himeji City in Hyogo prefecture. We have 198 beds and our hospital deals with an average of 661 patients every day. The average admission period is 11.3 days, and our hospital is, therefore, a typical mid-scale hospital in Japan. We constructed medical information support systems using the commercial database software FileMaker Pro. The areas addressed by our system are "Medical systems for patients", "Efficiency of duties", "Prevention of medical accidents", and "Secondary utilization of medical information". FileMaker Pro allows the control of large numbers of files, sufficient network functionality, ease of customization, connection to other database software *via* ODBC, and low cost of implementation. In addition, FileMaker Pro is commonly used by many medical staff in the hospital. Our system was integrated with other hospital systems, such as PACS, ordering systems, and part of the general account system.

Here, we introduce the development of our medical information support system.

The radiology system began the operation in July 2002.

The hospital system was first implemented in October 2002.

Patient attributes were obtained from the general account system in March 2003.

The PACS system was implemented in September 2003.

The examination system was first used in March 2004. The general account system was upgraded in July 2004.

The ordering system was implemented in November 2004.

In this way, the computerization system in our hospital was developed in a step-by-step manner (Table **1**).

Table 1: Development of the medical information support system

Jul 2002	Implementation of radiology system
Oct 2002	Implementation of hospital system
Mar 2003	Patient attributes were obtained
Sep 2003	Implementation of PACS system
Mar 2004	Implementation of examination system
Jul 2004	General account system was upgraded
Nov 2004	Implementation of ordering system

2. MATERIALS AND METHODS

The FileMaker system consists of three servers running FileMaker Server 5.5 and 70 clients running FileMaker 5.5 on Windows 2000 and Windows XP. By purchasing the *FM Box Set* software package, we can easily install all of the clients in the hospital at minimal cost.

The general account system consisted of 33 clients in July 2004. The network consisted of two local area networks (LANs), *i.e.*, the medical information LAN and the general account LAN, connected to the interface server. Our FileMaker databases consist of master databases containing data regarding patient attributes, drug information, disease information, blood type, infections, hospital calendar, address and post code, staff attributes, passwords, *etc.*, and operations databases consisting of administration schedules, clinical pathways [2], clinical histories, examination schedules, imaging reports, operation plans, staff shifts, programs for searching patient attributes and diseases, lists of asthma patients, *etc.,* [3] (Fig. **1**).

In addition, the FileMaker systems allow us to refer to connect the groupware server, DICOM server, and blood examination server. The ordering system has been developed in a step-by-step manner. First, we developed the examination reservation system for the Department of Radiology. Development was conducted by a systems engineer in the hospital in collaboration with the staff of the Information System Committee and the managers of all sections.

The FileMaker databases obtain patient attributes from the general account system every 3 min. Integration was achieved through the interface server that we developed. These servers were connected with ODBC. On the other hand, we export examination information to the general account systems.

After inputting the finish signal on the HIS system constructed using FileMaker Pro, the data are transferred to the interface server. The programs running on the general account systems obtain the data on a regular schedule. We developed only this interface server shown in Fig. **2**.

Figure 1: The operation databases.

3. RESULTS

After working this cooperation program, we could re-examine the operation of duties. This system allowed the rapid scheduling of operations and prevented non-payment of fees, *etc.* The system engineers and programmers collaborated closely with general system vendors and each department in the development cycle. The development process was fast because we added only interface servers to standard systems, and the costs were kept low because we used the standard resources at our hospital.

We conformed to the guidelines of IHE-J (Integrating the Healthcare Enterprise initiative in Japan), and achieved integration of this system with HIS, RIS, and PACS in the Department of Radiology of our hospital.

We can refer to the results of computed radiography (CR), computed tomography (CT), and magnetic resonance image (MRI) on any client in the hospital immediately by connecting to the FileMaker Pro system and DICOM server through a web browser.

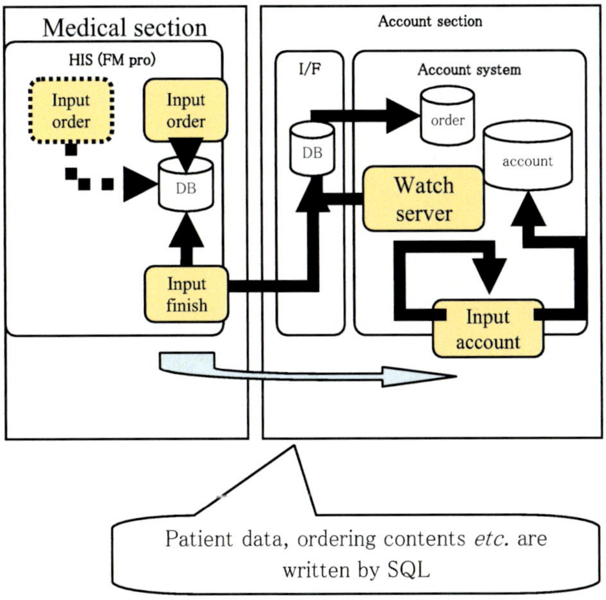

Figure 2: Cooperation systems.

RIS is organized by this FileMaker Pro system, which makes it easy to reserve examinations as necessary. On the other hand, patient information from the hospital system can be used automatically. The image report system is also convenient due to the immediate distribution of thumbnail images. This system will be useful for monitoring of medical information and for improving the quality of diagnosis and research (Fig. **3**).

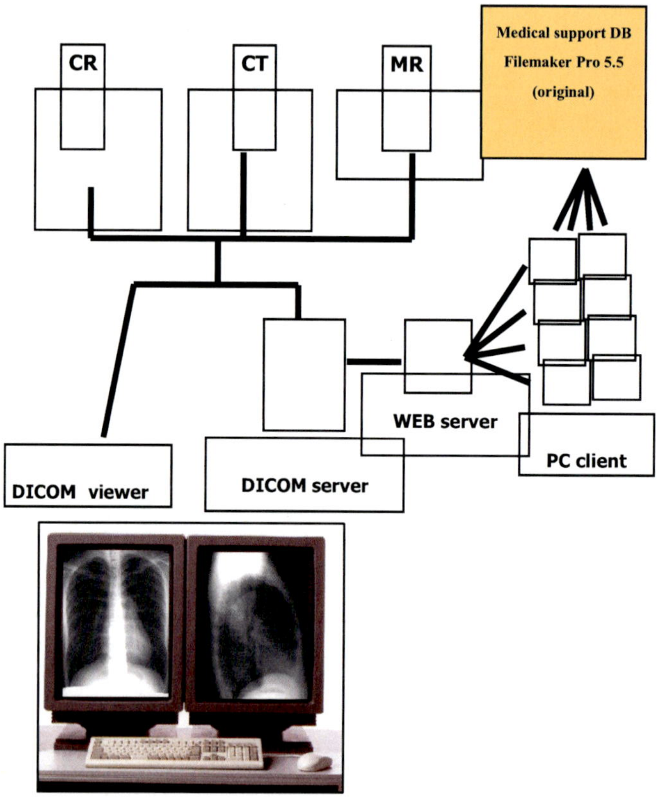

Figure 3: HIS-RIS-PACS.

4. DISCUSSION

The IHE-J guidelines are applied to the standards, such as HL7/DICOM, and specify the construction of medical information system with utilization of HIS, RIS, and PACS. Hospital systems are developed by multiple vendors. The IHE presents department of clinical image cooperates with every section according to HL7 [4, 5]. It is important to accumulate medical information to allow appropriate treatment of patients and to construct medical information systems for medical teams.

On the other hand, e-Japan introduced electronic medical records in more than 60% of large-scale hospitals with more than 400 beds by 2006. However, it is estimated that the spread of electronic medical records will remain at 10.9% among small-scale hospitals with less than 400 beds.

It is difficult for small-scale hospitals to introduce and maintain electronic medical records even with the aid of government subsidies because there are few direct economical merits of implementing such systems. Thus, the digital division between large- and small-scale hospitals will increase. Our medical information support system using FileMaker Pro has become a valuable information resource and fulfils the same functions as electronic medical records systems.

According to the recommendations of the IHE, an ideal hospital system will be capable of flexible cooperation with several other systems. Our medical information support system developed using FileMaker Pro is an ideal hospital system, because it can cooperate with other hospital systems as well as functioning as a standalone system.

This is not an electronic medical record system in the wide sense, but is suitable for deployment in small-scale hospitals because it has low costs and can be customized easily.

In future studies, we will integrate this system with the general account, drug ordering, and the electronic clinical pathway systems. Our medical information support system will become more useful, and may become an actual electronic medical record system in future. If our systems belonged to neighborhood area, there would be many precious properties.

CONFLICT OF INTEREST

None declared.

ACKNOWLEDGEMENT

None declared.

REFERENCES

[1] Yoshida S, Nakamura T, Mimasu S, *et al.* Toward the solution for digital divide in medical field. Japan Society for Health Care Management 2003; 4: 519-524.
[2] Yoshida S, Mimasu S, Taniguchi J, *et al.* Database of patients using FileMaker Pro. Japan Pediatric Society 1999; 103: 287.
[3] Nakamura T, Yoshida S. The effect of the introduction of IT systems. Media Select 2003; 68-69.
[4] JIRA Industries Association of Radiological Systems http://www.jira-net.or.jp/ihe-jp
[5] The Official Homepage of HEALTH LEVEL SEVEN, JAPAN http://www.hl7.jp.

CHAPTER 7

Gradual Implementation of Local Medical Information System Within Hospital Using FileMaker Pro®: New Insights on Physician and Clinical Stuff Adaptation

Kazutoshi Matsunami*

Matsunami General Hospital, 185-1 Tashiro, Kasamatsu, Hashima-Gun, Gifu, Japan

Abstract: The Matsunami General Hospital (434 beds, aiming acute management of diseases and injuries) looks ahead to the next century with excitement and enthusiasm, eager to build upon its past strengths and to continue to develop new ways for serving its patients and the improvement of public health, in particular Gifu area. This chapter introduces the application of FileMaker Pro® in intra-hospital clinical supporting system (CSS) to give new insights on physician, medical stuffs and patients. The FileMaker Pro-associated local networks cost are reasonable and they are easy to be incorporated into non-governed hospital.

Keywords: FileMaker Pro, electronic health record, end user computing, clinical supporting system, user-made medical IT system, medical information system, local area network, diagnosis procedure combination, iPad, hospital information system, data ware house.

1. INTRODUCTION

The electronic medical record (EMR) may improve health care delivery by facilitating physicians' communication about medications, enhancing documentation, increasing efficiency, and fostering information sharing and responsibility with patients. Implementation is often costly, takes time and computer expertise, and has unanticipated consequences. Concerns include its negative influence on the physician-patient encounter, altering the patient's narrative in documentation, reducing patient-centeredness, and affecting medical decision making and the physician-patient relationship [1]. Even though, empirical studies of the EMR have increased, underscoring the physical room layout and how consultation computers are "more than just pieces of furniture", few mixed

***Address correspondence to Kazutoshi Matsunami:** Department of Gynecology, Matsunami General Hospital, Japan; E-mail: mgh2@matsunami-hsp.or.jp

Shunji Wakamiya, Kazunobu Yamauchi and Hiroyuki Yoshihara (Eds)

methods inquiries have explored the impact of EMRs on actual clinical encounters, patients' perspectives, and physicians' adaptive strategies. Nation-specific challenges, such as fee-for-service environments, may pose barriers to EMR implementation. A Kuwaiti example reports the experiences of clerical staff regarding EMR implementation [2]. Although, the impact of EMRs on physician-patient communication is controversial, more investigation is needed to compare EMR with non-EMR environments. Finally, longitudinal and holistic approaches to this subject are rare [1].

We report the application of FileMaker Pro® in intra-hospital clinical supporting system (CSS) to give new insights on physician, medical stuffs and patients.

2. OVERVIEW OF MATSUNAMI GENERAL HOSPITAL

Beds: 434

Outpatients: 856.5 (daily, 2009)

Average inpatients stay: 13.5 days (2009)

Department: Internal Medicine (General, Respiratory, Gastroenterology, Nephrology, Endocrinology, Neurology, Infectious Diseases, Collagen Diseases); Gastroenterological Surgery, General Surgery; Heart Center (Cardiovascular Internal Medicine, Cardiovascular Surgery); Breast Center (Breast Surgery); Thoracic Surgery; Orthopedic Surgery; Ambulatory Care Center for Children (Pediatrics, Pediatric Surgery); Dermatology; Plastic & Reconstructive Surgery; Comprehensive Women's Medicine (General Obstetrics, Gynecological Surgery); Reproductive Surgery; Urology; Ophthalmology; Neurosurgery; Emergency Medical Care Center; Interventional Radiology; Anesthesiology; Rehabilitation.

Number of staff: Doctors: 92 (incl. 12 interns), Nurses: 359, Pharmacists: 26, Medical technicians: 86, Nurse Assistants: 51, Administration: 311, Registered volunteers: 15.

3. CHARACTERISTICS OF FILEMAKER Pro®

FileMaker Pro is powerful, easy-to-use database software that helps us and our team to get any task done faster. Millions of people in business, government, and education use FileMaker Pro to effortlessly manage all their information on Windows, Mac, and the web [3]. In addition to more than 30 built-in Starter Solutions that help us manage our important tasks, FileMaker Pro also has more easy-to-use tools to enable you in Japanese.

4. NECESSITY OF NEW SYSTEM OF OUR OWN COMPOSITION

We introduce the present conditions of our medical information system. Our Hospital Information System (HIS) adopts Clinical Information System (CIS) of IBM as an ordering system and performs orders such as examination and drugs, and provides filmless radiological image with Picture Archiving and Communication Systems (PACS). The images are visible at any monitors within hospital (Fig. **1**). Fig. **2** shows monitor-view of our local net work. However, we use non-electronic clinical record with paper.

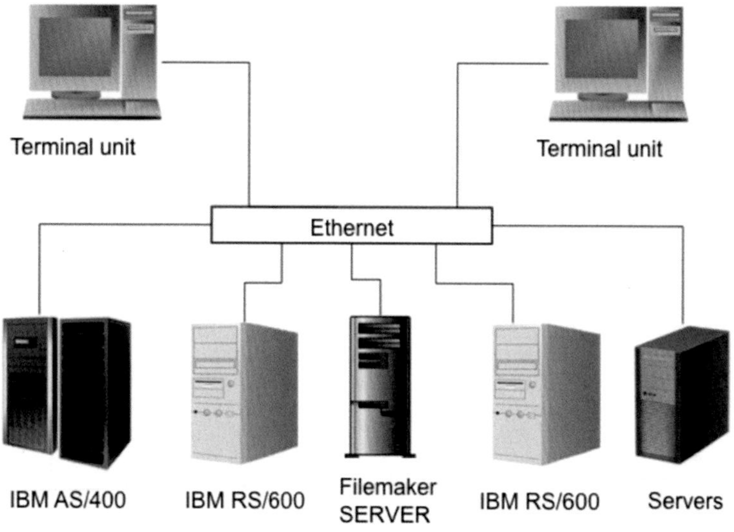

Figure 1: Local net work of Matsunami General Hospital and its branch Matsunami Health Care Clinic.

A format of a clinical record depends on each department. All documents including hospitalization, discharge and insurance providers were hand-written by separate formatting which is necessary for the department. The doctor arranged medical summary, operative records, medical certificates, various requests book in a freehand drawing. Only problem and medication lists were recorded in the

EMR. The hospital laboratory software was used for laboratory data without communication between systems. Except for 2 early adopters who used a laptop computer during consultations, other physicians recorded patients' histories in the paper chart. Physicians frequently left the consultation rooms for laboratory and test results and to update clinical lists and prescriptions. Sitting facing the patient, physicians usually place the paper chart on their laps to read and record notes, some look at the patient, others at chart, some stay silent, and others read aloud while writing. Although, physicians observed eye contact with patients varied, patients generally expressed satisfaction in exit interviews.

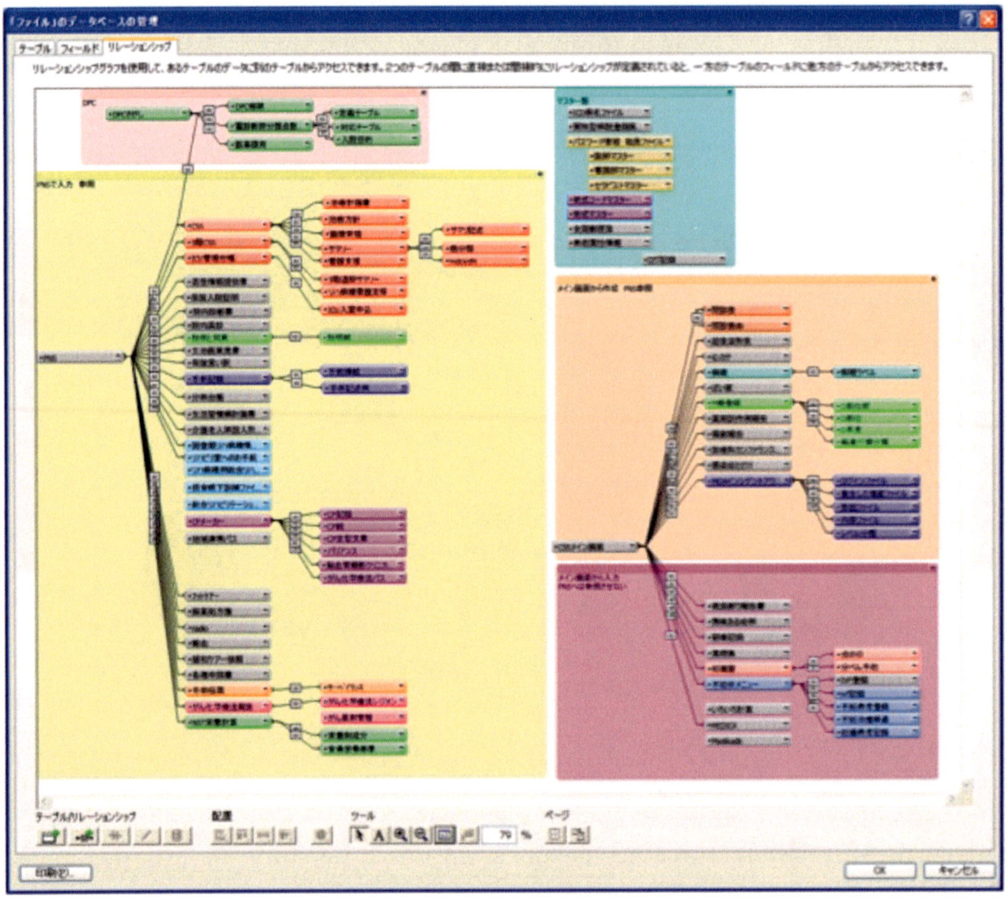

Figure 2: Monitor-view of local net work of Matsunami General Hospital.

Doctors were pleasantly surprised by the ease of referrals: "Everybody was nervous. but then when we started doing it, we all loved it". Nurse's aides worried about their inadequate typing abilities and children's potential destructiveness. Nurses feared short-term double work. One said, "We'll always have the record though. And we will no longer have to worry, you know, they can't find it". As did staff members, patients expressed positive perceptions about speed and access and concerns about security. Some patients were more computer savvy than the health care personnel. Some patients indicated neutrality whether documentation was electronic or written.

Patients were also concerned about security, regardless of personal computer experience. One man wanted file protection because the "computer cannot be something to rely on. it can steal all the information", whereas a 32-year-old woman said, "I'm fine just as long as nobody else gets (the files) besides doctors".

We have introduced an electronic chart in this phase, but, in addition, the system which we could be satisfied with was seen off in the dot of cost effectiveness without being found.

As for me, the basic significance of existence of an electronic chart extracts a necessary thing in medical information of enormous quantity and analyzes it and thinks that we contribute to the medical quality improvement. The given electronic chart is insufficient with the aspect, and it is the product in which a word processor and graph making software were incorporated in an ordering system, if we talk in a fiercely. It is not easy to extract the necessary data from enormous data. Therefore, firstly we set necessary data and decided to accumulate only the data.

We set up this system on reasonable price so that database that we can accumulate and share the necessary data within this hospital. Sharing paper chart information was verbal while the chart remained out of the patient's visual range. Although, during the transition physicians rarely shared patient information on the computer, they often share information on the screen after the implementation. The researcher's notes read: "Physician calls patient to the screen and shows her the labs uses the cursor to direct the patient (saying), 'Don't look at me, look at this—the lab results". At study's end the researcher witnessed a physician sharing the paper chart with the patient.

5. WHY FILEMAKER Pro?

As described above, it is easy to incorporate FileMaker Pro in marketed database management system most, and it is evaluated when there is system construction without expertise; we use the card-type database version from version 2. Version 6 now works in our hospital. In addition, FileMaker Pro contains the charm merits, easy layout-setting in Japanese and immediate starting-up in Japanese. Many Japanese medical staffs including doctors anticipate the Japanese Society for User-Made Medical IT System (J-SUMMITS), a group of the user of the software. A system by FileMaker Pro plays an important role as a system burying an electronic chart and an on-site gap in electronic chart induction Hospital.

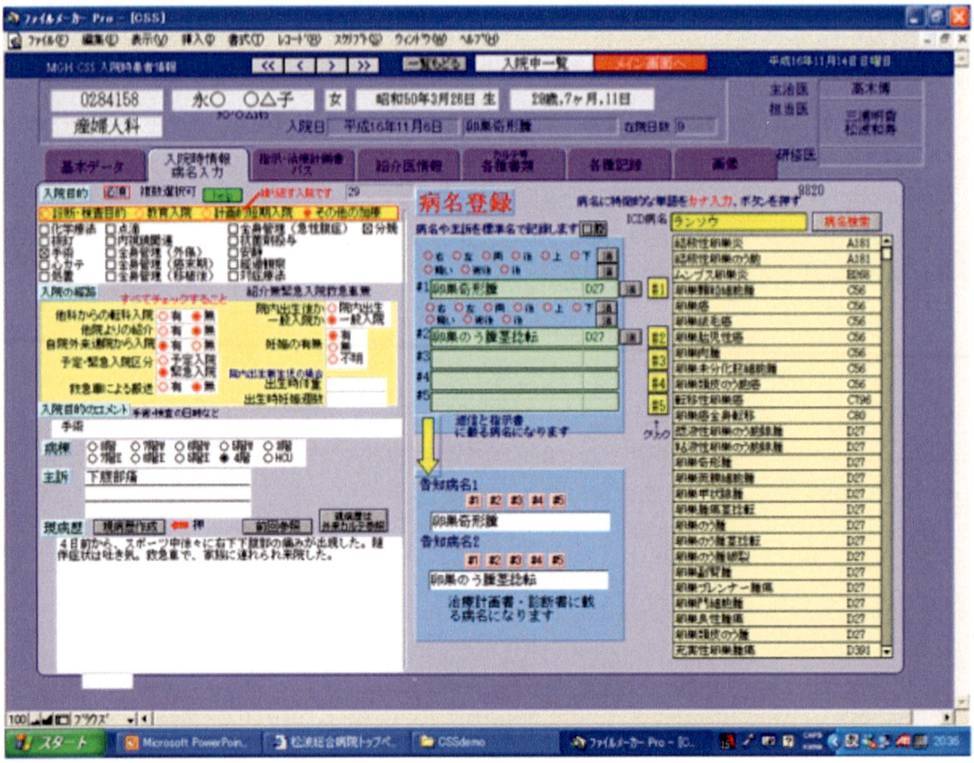

Figure 3: Monitor-view of basic information of the patient.

6. CONTENTS OF A SYSTEM

Document making, as illustrated in Figs. **3-5**, there are clinical pathway, medical care reporting book, a medical certificate, an insurance medical certificate, a consultation request book, an informed consent book, discharge summary, nursery summary, rehabilitation request, a family doctor opinion book, operation note, a childbirth record, an ICU account book, and cancer registration. They contribute DPC coding, incident report, infectious disease report, bedsore report, collection of achievements, and clinical conference record.

Physicians adapted to the system use by body position, computer placement, verbal references to the computer, and how they shared information with patients. Physicians appeared to try to decrease computer intrusiveness. The computer could still create unpleasant surprises, such as delayed log-ins, frozen screens, and computer crashes.

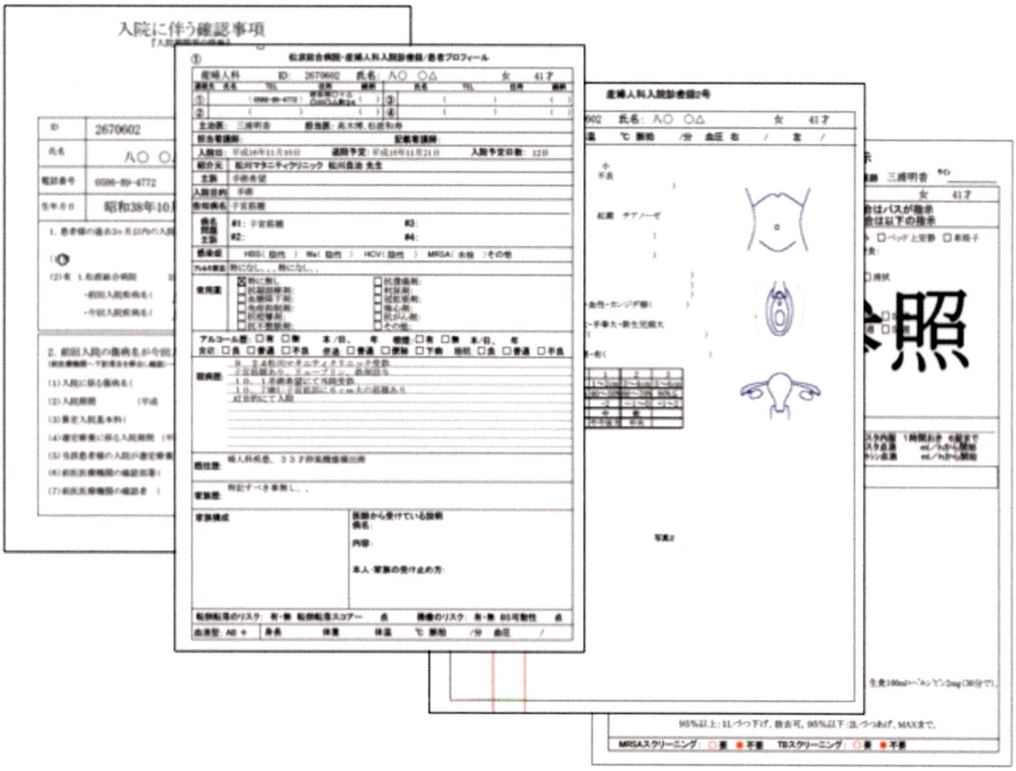

Figure 4: Monitor-view of general physical findings, hospitalization *etc.*

Physicians made explicit computer references, sometimes apologizing for computer awkwardness. During the transition, physicians would commonly sit facing the patient with the chart on their lap, stand to examine the patient, then sit to discuss the findings. With implementation, physicians increasingly turned the computer monitor so the patient could view it more easily and alternated looking at the computer screen with maintaining patient eye contact.

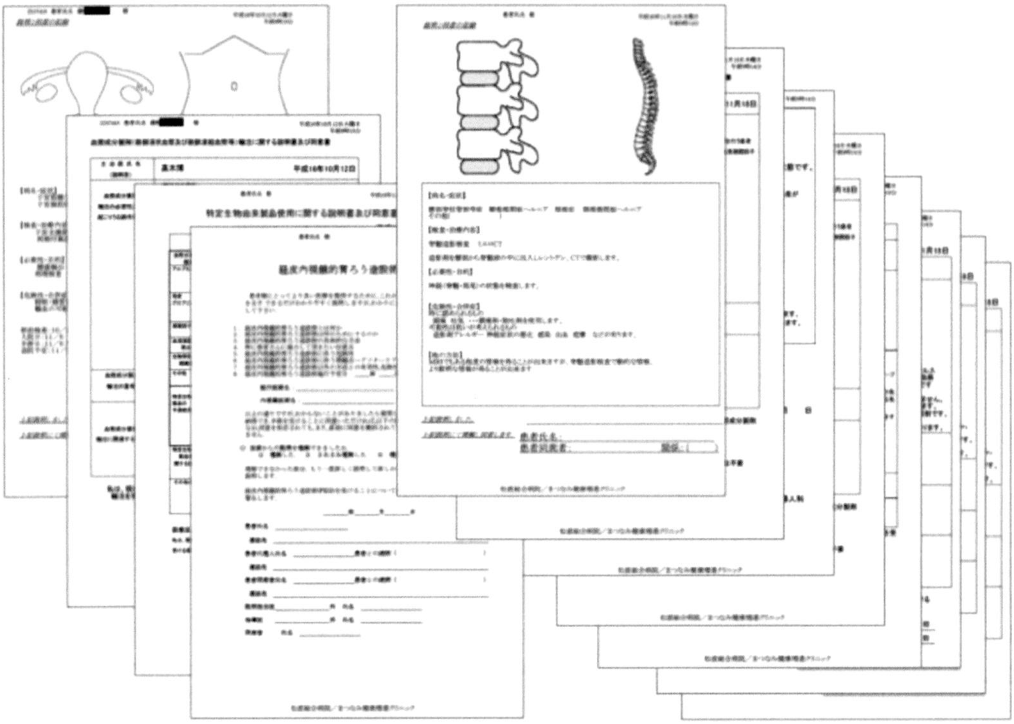

Figure 5: Monitor-view of anesthesia request, an operation request an NST request, a relaxation care request.

Nonverbal strategies were then frequent. One physician, with an immovable keyboard and monitor before him, stretched his arm back towards the patient on the examination table, creating a symbolic link with the patient whom he could not face directly. Others extended a leg or angled knees towards the patient sitting beside the computer. When the patient was on the examination table, the physicians' knees were often awkwardly perpendicular to the patient, while the physician's body faced the computer with back to the patient. We recruit data in DWH (Data Ware House) from HIS *(Hospital Information System*) in many institutions, and methods to use are fine for FileMaker Pro. Methods to take in HIS as documents such as PDF (Portable Document Format) have the information that occurred in FileMaker Pro side stolen. Fig. **6** shows these networks.

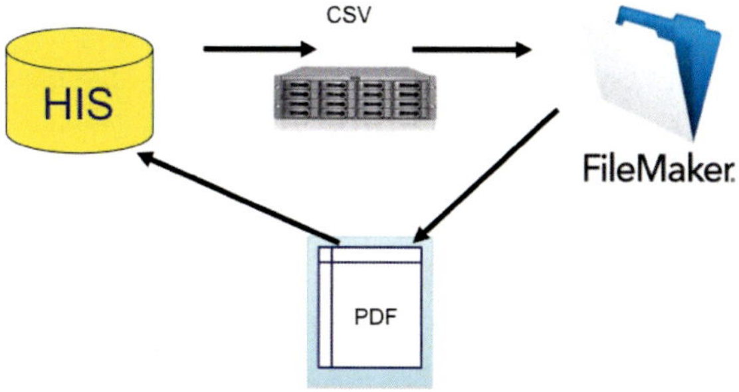

Figure 6: Schematic proposal on HIS *(Hospital Information System)*, pdf (Portable Document Format), CSV (Comma Separated Values) and FileMaker Pro linkages.

7. LIMITATIONS AND FUTURE PROSPECTS

As electronic medical records became integrated in this setting, concerns about deleterious consequences of electronic medical record implementation were ameliorated, positive outcomes were realized, and unexpected benefits were revealed. The choice of where in the room the computer is placed and its role as a third actor alters the physician-patient interaction in a major way. We document how initially awkward physicians boosted their confidence with time and became more adept. As others have noted, physicians accommodated through body language, introductions to the electronic medical record, excuses for computer set-up delay, monitor positioning for collaborative viewing, invitations for patients to sit closer, and references to the computer as a shared burden [4]. Repeating patients' words while typing signaled physician attention and allowed time for correction by this "pausing". Just-in-time information and referrals added to efficient work flows and accompanied increased sharing of the electronic medical record with the patient in contrast to the physicians' not sharing the paper chart before electronic medical record implementation. Though electronic medical record multitasking may be burdensome, adjustment was noteworthy because few physicians were early electronic medical record adopters. This adaptation supports the recommendations for preparatory discussion and gradual implementation [5].

Participating patients may have been more satisfied with their physicians than those who declined participation. Conducting exit interviews within the clinic (albeit in private rooms) may have inhibited patient criticism. Although, anthropological observation contains some subjective aspects, the use of one researcher and a standard observation form and interview guide provided a uniform record to increase rigor. Extensive discussions by the analysis team facilitated consideration of alternate interpretations of findings.

Lastly, we remake it with new version 11 while referring to an existing file to structural rearranging and security reinforcement. This reinforcement can also put application of ESS above mentioned iPad and iPhone and other version of FileMaker. Curricula for this system training are clearly necessary. In addition, physicians should learn to type well before moving to the system and be trained to improve communication. Computer placement in the consultation room should be considered, as it affects the patients' inclusivity or openness during the physician-patient interaction. Further study should focus on how the patient record is shared; increased patient access to the patient record may lead to decreased physician authority, yet it may also enhance the physician-patient partnership and patient responsibility. Further outcomes research may also be warranted to examine the effects of EMR use on health and disease. In this population, our results justified the considerable expense, time, and effort expended. It is highly plausible that similar results could be obtained in comparable settings.

CONFLICT OF INTEREST

None declared.

ACKNOWLEDGEMENT

None declared.

REFERENCES

[1] Shield R, Goldman R, Anthony D, Wang N, Doyler R, Borkan J. Gradual electronic health record implementation: new insights on physician and patient adaptation. Ann Fam Med 2010 8:316-326.

[2] Al-Azmi S, Al-Enezi N, Chowdhury R. Users' attitudes to an electronic medical record system and its correlates: a multivariate analysis. HIM J 2009 38:33-40.

[3] MICRISOFT. http://www.filemaker.com/. (2010.8.24)

[4] Crosson J, Stroebel C, Scott J, Stello B, Crabtree B. Implementing an electronic medical record in a family medicine practice: communication, decision making, and conflict. Ann Fam Med 2005 3:307-311.

[5] Nemeth L, Feifer C, Stuart G, Ornstein S. Implementing change in primary care practices using electronic medical records: a conceptual framework. Implement Sci 2008 3:3.

CHAPTER 8

A Medical Information Management System by Medics, For Medics, Built With Filemaker and Incorporated into the Hospital Information System

Shinsuke Hiramatsu*

Nippon Steel Hirohata Hospital, 3-1 Yumesaki, Hirohata-Ku, Himeji, Hyogo, Japan

Abstract: Electronic medical records or hospital information system (HIS) is designed to collect individual patients' information in the clinic. Otherwise conducting medical research, requires the collection of information, and the current HIS is not considered for this. Also, there is no such mechanism to be easily summarized the patient's history in the list form.

In Nippon Steel Hirohata hospital, we build and run the subsystem powered by Filemaker, the commercial database software, by the method of end user computing for 18 years.

In the subsystem, we create the ledger of hospitalization, surgical register, and list of malignant tumor patients, and any medical information. Also this supports to make the hospital certificates and other documentation. In addition, we are making the integrated clinical history system on those systems. This information is referred by all devices on the network in our hospital, which helps with the effective use of information shared by each department.

Keywords: Filemaker, EUC, certification, cancer registration, patient history, management, connection with HIS, admission record, discharge summary, cancer treatment, regimen, drug information, ICD-10.

1. WHAT TYPE OF TOOL IS IT?

There are many hospitals that are introducing hospital information systems (HIS) every year. However, these systems are not necessarily supporting and reducing the workload of medical staff. In fact, there are many who say that it creates more work, or that it is complicated to use. I believe that the reason for this lies in the

***Address correspondence to Shinsuke Hiramatsu:** Department of Obstetrics and Gynecology, Nippon Steel Hirohata Hospital, Japan; E-mail: s_hiramatsu@hirohata-hp.or.jp fact that HIS was not initially designed with the aim of supporting medical professionals in mind. In other words, the HIS was designed to collect individual patients' information, but lateral information handling was left out of the picture. For example, when you want the patient list of a certain disease you are examining, it cannot be easily obtained.

Since 1993, Nippon Steel Hirohata Hospital in Himeji Japan, has been utilizing commercially available database software called Filemaker to construct an information system to assist medical examinations [1].

Four Power Mac G5s are used as server machines while Filemaker Server 5.5 runs 24 hours a day. Furthermore, two XServe G5s which run MacOS X server are available as backup.

There are 470 client computers powered by Windows XP that are already used for HIS, as well as computers running Mac OS X which are installed in the doctors' offices.

There are over 250 files whose volume surpasses 1 GB. The largest file contains over 3,000,000 records.

2. WHAT TYPE OF CONTENT DOES IT HAVE?

Since 1993, basic patient information and names of illnesses were synchronized in order to assist in the writing of prescriptions and the creation of medical certificates.

Following this, we introduced online surgical operation appointments, and, based on that information, created an operation management record.

From 1997 onwards, we made the change from hand-writing to computer printing the top page of hospital admission records. That information is used to create a hospital admission management record. Furthermore, we have started to use the system to assist in creating hospital discharge summary reports. At the same time, a pregnancy/delivery management record was created for the obstetrics department. Later, these databases became a patient history management record, and with added ICD coding and a standardized statistical function, we developed this record into a patient history management system.

In addition, we compiled a database of drugs in use at the hospital, collected information on each one, and shared it online. That list is developing into a drug inventory management system.

From 1998, we started registering cancer patient records. It is possible to input the name of the condition, pathological diagnosis, stage classification, treatment history, and outpatient examination history. It has information-registering capabilities which follow government outlines, and a registration slip can be created directly from the information in the system.

Organization of chemotherapy regimens is also included in the system. The hospital's Chemotherapy Committee registers the regimen, and a treatment schedule is created. A treatment calendar may be created by entering the treatment date and dosage. At the same time, a sheet of dosage instructions is automatically created.

Furthermore, the system has started supporting outpatient clinic examinations. The system organizes the information for outpatient examinations and acts as a portal for admission management records, pregnancy/delivery management records, and cancer patient management records.

In 2000, we added a supplemental function which aims to assist medical examinations and treatment by creating clinical pathways utilizing paper. This is an excellent system that allows synchronization of multiple flows based on admission date and operation dates. Furthermore, by selecting and organizing daily nursing care created in the clinical pathway, the system can create a nursing care worksheet in the hospital wards.

In 2005, when we updated the HIS to Fujitsu Hope/EG Main FX [2], we linked information on hospital admission and release and surgical operation appointment information. Finally, Diagnosis Procedure Combination (DPC) information was also linked, enabling medical staff to acquire accurate information on medical examination and treatment.

3. HOW TO CONNECT WITH HIS

All information is entered as it occurs. Within that information, multiple data such as patient attributes, condition, patient transfer, surgical operation appointments, DPC, blood type, and the existence of any infectious disease, are all linked to the sub-system.

Patient attribute information is entered in the medical account system, which is linked to HIS, and is also linked to the sub-system in the same way (Fig.**1**).

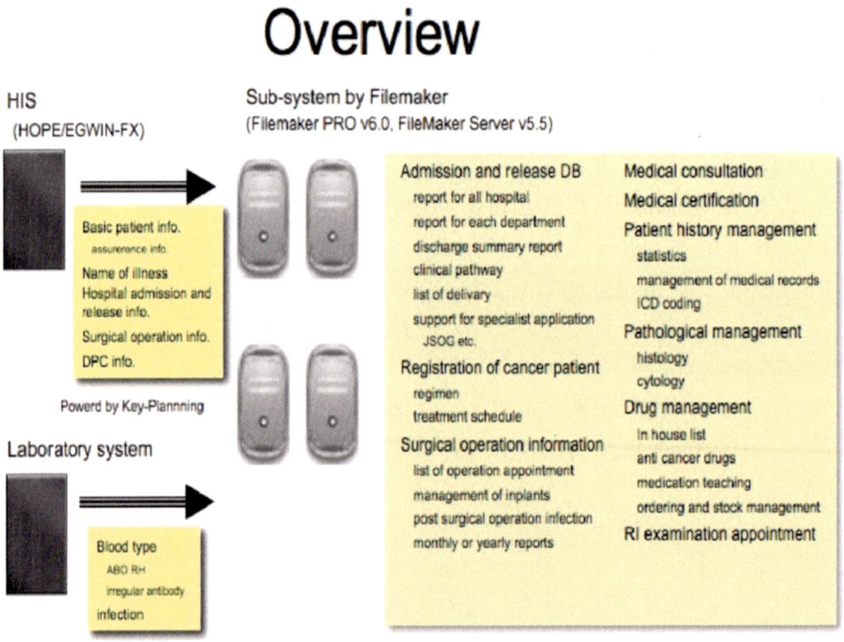

Figure 1: Overview of HIS and FileMaker subsystem.

Information on condition, patient attributes, surgical operation appointments, and DPC are entered in the HIS, which are linked to surrounding systems such as the medical account system, RIS, and the pharmacological work system, and flow to the sub-system in the same way. From the HIS or the medical account system, text-based information is sent by socket communication and received by individual Java applets in the Mac OS X. The applets use Filemaker 6.0's web connection to send the information into intermediate files in Filemaker. Filemaker interprets the information and updates the corresponding databases [3].

Information on blood type and infectious disease tests, on confirmation of lab results, are output by CSV text. File-maker collates and imports these texts and makes updates on a daily basis.

There is also a function within the HIS that allows data which can be exported to the clipboard, such as the test results of individual patients, to be linked using the clipboard. Test results which are exported to the clipboard in a text format from the HIS are pasted into the database with File-maker and organized for later use.

Results from some examination machines, including ultrasound machines, are also linked. GE Voluson E8 allows results to be sent to a dedicated application in Windows XP by socket communication and saved as a tagged text file. The file is then imported with File-maker.

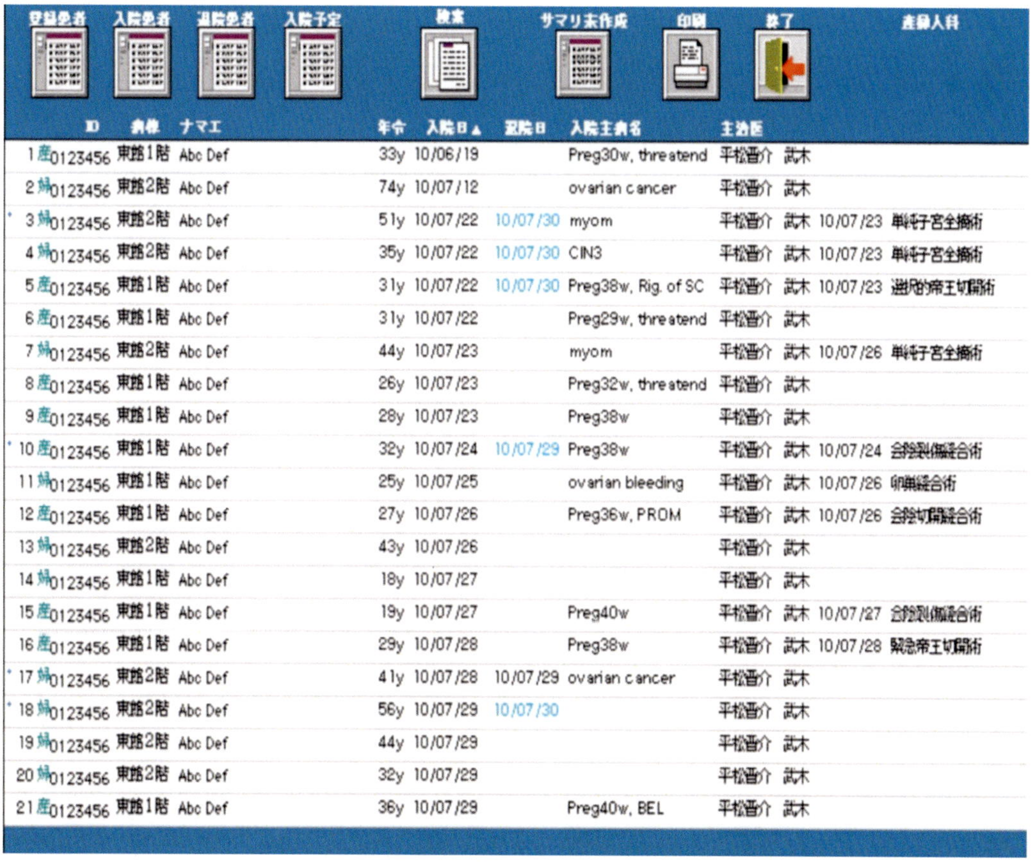

Figure 2: Patient list in charge, move to Fig. **3** of Input form by one click.

4. METHODS OF USE AND RESULTS SHOWN

4.1. Hospital Admission Management Record and Patient History Management System

The life histories of individual patients - such as their complaints at outpatient visits, current medical conditions, past conditions, childbirth history, and smoking history - are compiled and saved. This information is the basis of all medical diagnosis and treatment. This information is shared by all hospital departments, which eliminates the need for the same information to be repeatedly entered. Because information acquired from past diagnoses and treatments can also be put to practical use, it is possible to create an intelligence database with no gaps (Figs. **2**, **3**).

This record is connected to all other records; therefore, information may be entered from here directly into the cancer patient record, the pregnancy and delivery management record, *etc.*

The greatest practical use of this system is the hospital admission/release record which utilizes hospital admission and release information. This record becomes the foundation data for keeping tabs on the hospital's inpatients. Currently, medical examination records on inpatients are documented on the paper, but the summary of the patient being discharged from hospital is created on the aforementioned hospital admission/release record. Part of this information comes from information gathered from outpatient visits and/or from the contact card for the anaesthetist when an appointment for a surgical operation is made. Furthermore, in cases in which treatment requires that the patient be repeatedly admitted and released from hospital, information from the prior summary can be used to create a new summary. This serves the purpose of both improving the accuracy of information and eliminating duplicated data entry. For in-hospital cancer treatment, information created by the regimen is copied on to the hospital release report to create an accurate record. This hospital release report includes information on hospital admission/release as well as DPC, which are transferred to the patient history management system, and becomes the basic information for managing hospital release files and hospital statistics (Fig.**4**).

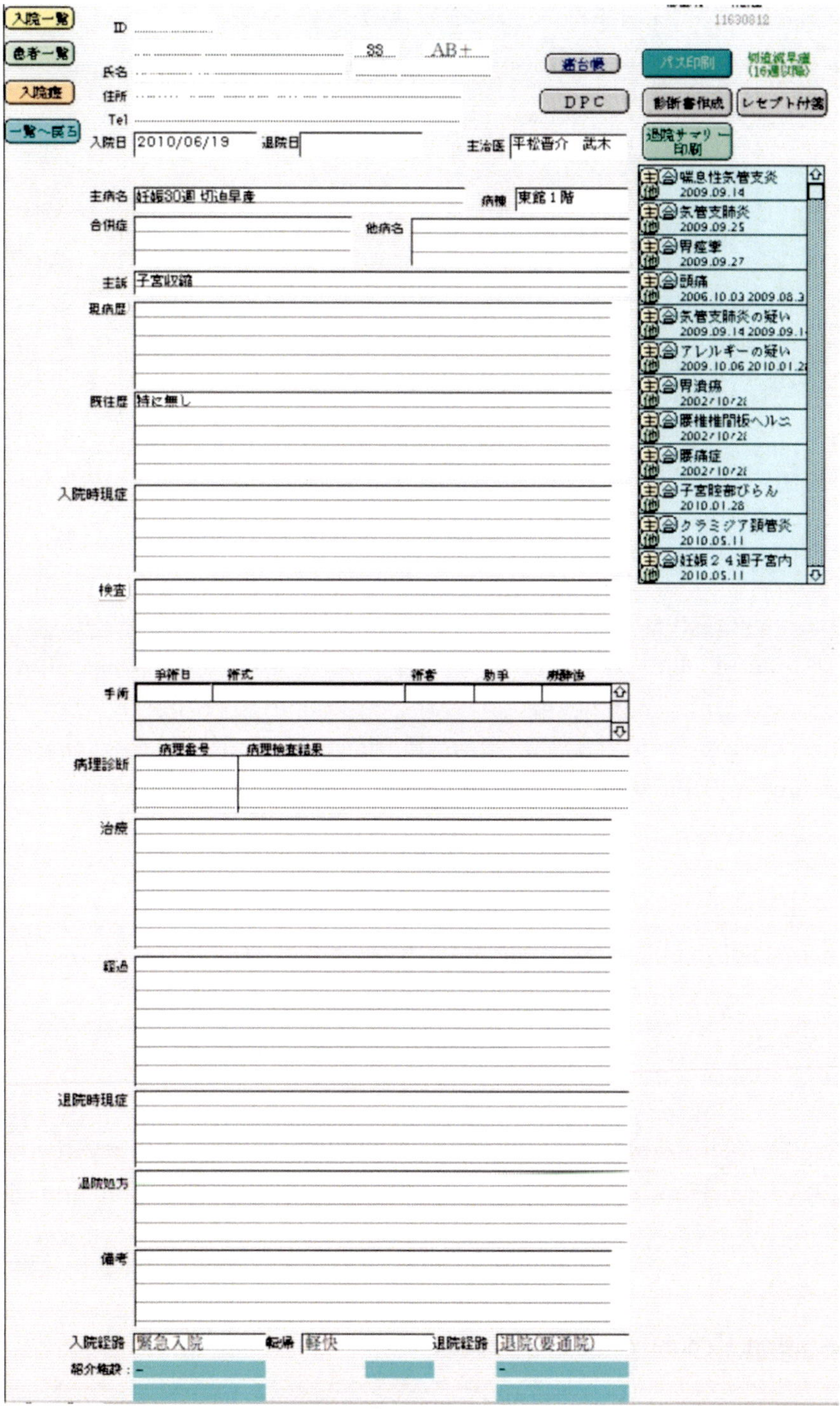

Figure 3: Input form of admission/release record.

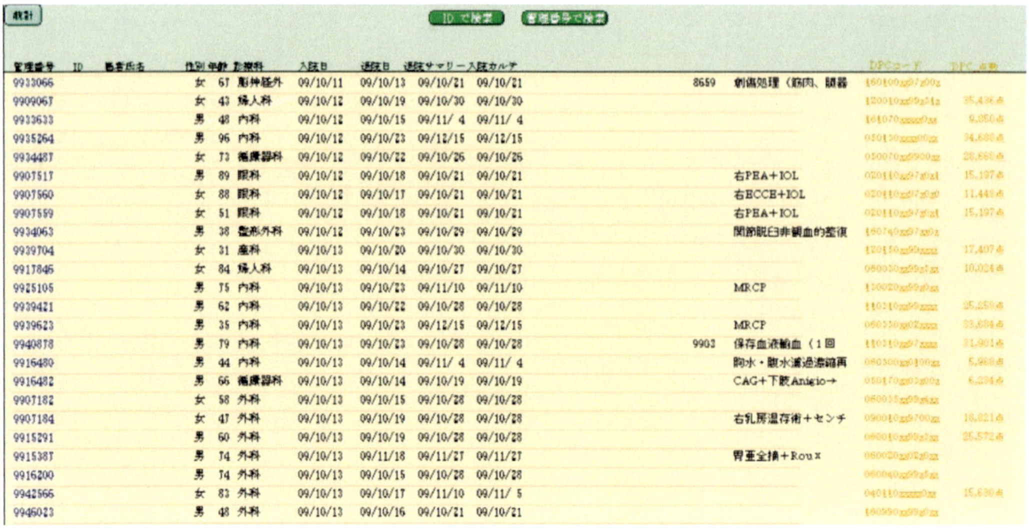

Figure 4: Patient list of medical history management.

The patient history management system created by File-maker is also original. Its statistical function has more functions than other applications available on the market. For example, patient statistics can be divided up region by region in order to create community-based statistics. Furthermore, the system has excellent augmentation ability which allows the user to create new statistics in a short space of time when necessary.

We think that it is best to think of all these separate data as one. Data regarding patients' medical history and life history in particular are the more precise: adding to the information collected in the past will improve overall accuracy. Furthermore, the handling of information when creating reports can have a great effect on eliminating unnecessary wasting of time.

Moreover, by being able to create a link with the patient history management system, the admission management record becomes more accurate, and, by using feedback from medical care record management specialists, the accuracy of hospital release summaries may also be improved (Fig. **5**).

4.2. Operation Records

Operation appointment information is also managed by File-maker. When an operation appointment is made with HIS, its information is transferred to Filemaker. The surgery department uses that information to schedule operations. With File-maker's flexibility, rescheduling, distributing schedules, and other original functions can be done with just one touch of a button.

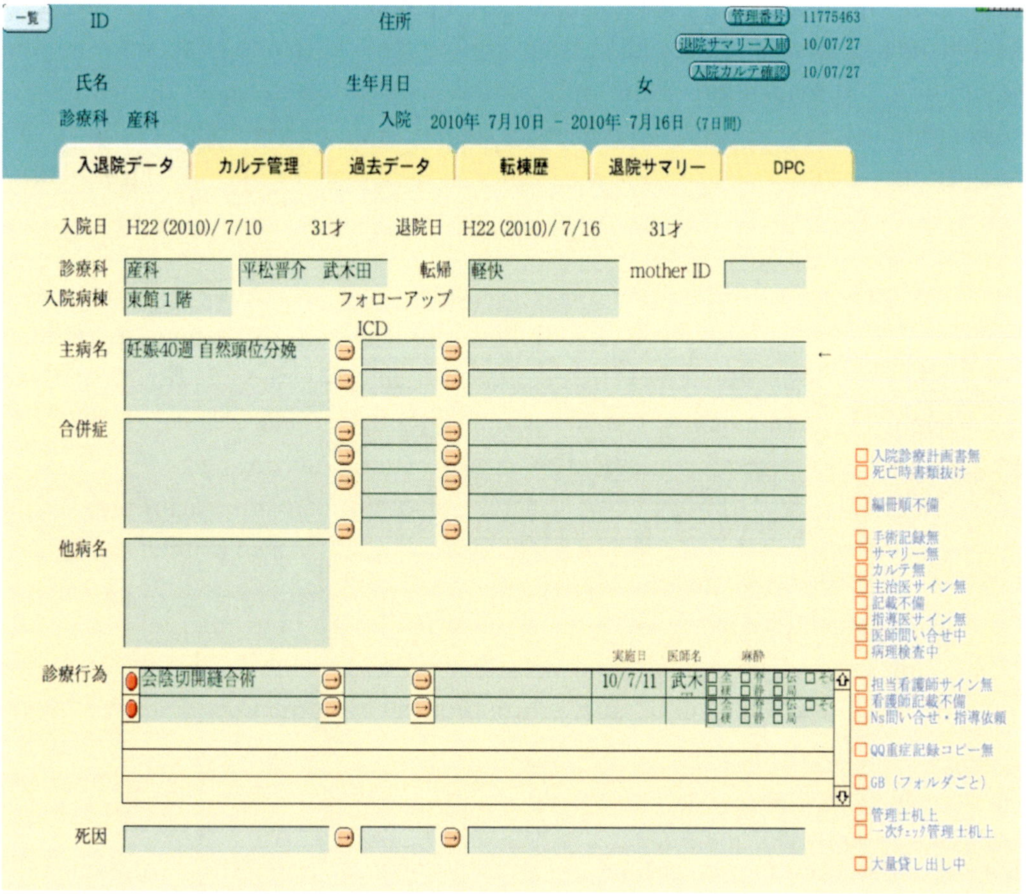

Figure 5: Medical history management of each patient.

At the same time, File-maker creates a contact card for the anaesthetist from the surgeon. Necessary information is imported from outpatient care, test results are copied *via* the clipboard from HIS, and the card is made in no time without a single error. Furthermore, information is directly sent from each doctor's office to a printer installed in the surgery department, eliminating the time and effort taken for transportation. This record can be consulted by all departments, and by being able to see at a glance the status of appointment schedules and the creation of anaesthetist cards, this acts as a great mutual information link.

4.3. Pregnancy and Childbirth Management Record

Pregnancy of course requires consistent observation from outpatient care through to in-hospital care. During pregnancy, information from the initial visit, to first/second trimester test results, fetal development, imaging, and the mother's health make for an extremely extensive list of chronological information. Compiling and managing all the information would be extremely difficult for a standard electronic record. A database run by File-maker, which allows for detailed and intricate control, allows a centralized management of the information.

In this record, the expected due date is determined from the information collected from the early stages of pregnancy. A corresponding pregnancy calendar and a label that includes a barcode for linking information to various peripheral machines are also created [4]. Fetal information gathered by ultrasound sonography is automatically transferred to File-maker and shown as a graph. Furthermore, the system automatically outputs material according to the mother's week of pregnancy. During inpatient care, outpatient care information is neatly organized for easier reference, and a foetal growth graph is also printed.

Moreover, after information regarding the birth of the child is entered, the system creates all sorts of documents and a birth certificate. Due to the fact that the system integrates the continuous chronological information gathered from outpatient visits all the way to birth and release from hospital, it is both labour-saving and extremely efficient.

Furthermore, information gathered regarding the actual birth is divided into information on the mother's condition and on the newborn baby. That information is linked to and registered with the newborn care department's database, and thus the flow of information is managed (Figs. **6**, **7**).

4.4. Cancer Patients Record

Cancer treatment can take an extremely long time, and so there is a need for the long-term management of information. The cancer patient is registered either through outpatient records or through hospital admission record. Registered information is in accordance with the Ministry of Health, Labour and Welfare guidelines. Thus, a record file for cancer registration can be created (Figs. **8**, **9**).

B-Scope	体重	CRL		BPD		FTA		FL		EFBW	
09.09.24	7w3d	11.7mm	0.8SD								
09.10.08	9w3d	27.9mm	0.9SD								
09.11.05	13w3d			27.4mm	0.5SD						
09.12.24	20w3d 49.3kg			49.5mm	-0.1SD			30.8mm	-0.3SD		
10.01.21	24w3d 52.1kg			58.3mm	-1.2SD			41.4mm	-0.2SD		
10.02.04	26w3d 52kg			64.1mm	-1.2SD	33.0mm	-1.1SD	45.3mm	-0.5SD	862g	-1.3SD
10.02.18	28w3d 52.7kg			71.2mm	-0.6SD	45.8mm	0.2SD	48.4mm	-1.0SD	1237g	-0.5SD
10.03.04	30w3d 52.9kg			77.8mm	-0.2SD	47.4mm	-0.8SD	56.6mm	0.5SD	1538g	-0.5SD
10.03.11	31w3d 52.7kg			77.6mm	-0.9SD	51.9mm	-0.7SD	57.2mm	0.0SD	1634g	-0.8SD
10.03.18	32w3d 53.9kg			82.2mm	-0.2SD	58.2mm	-0.2SD	57.7mm	-0.4SD	1883g	-0.4SD
10.03.25	33w3d 54.7kg			84.8mm	-0.1SD	59.0mm	-0.6SD	59.4mm	-0.5SD	2002g	-0.6SD
10.04.08	35w3d 55.8kg			88.1mm	-0.2SD	69.6mm	-0.2SD	66.2mm	0.6SD	2482g	-0.1SD

Figure 6: Fetal growth measurement.

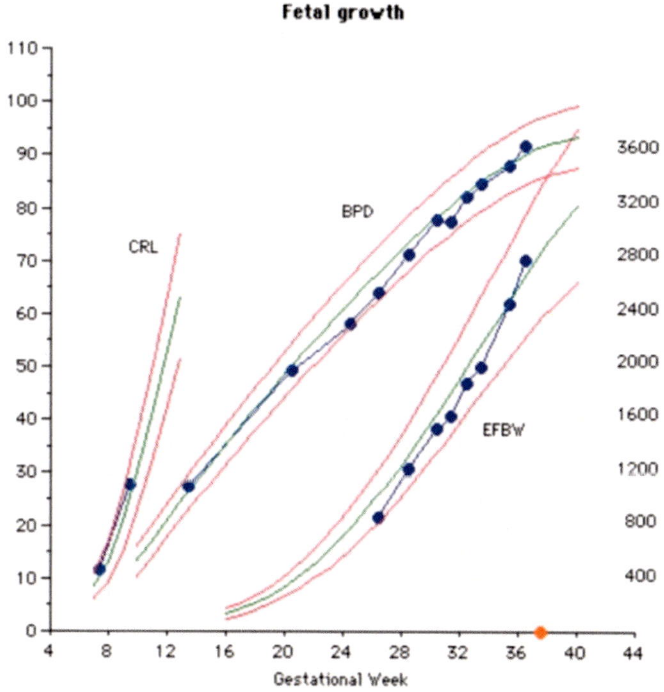

Figure 7: Fetal growth in graph.

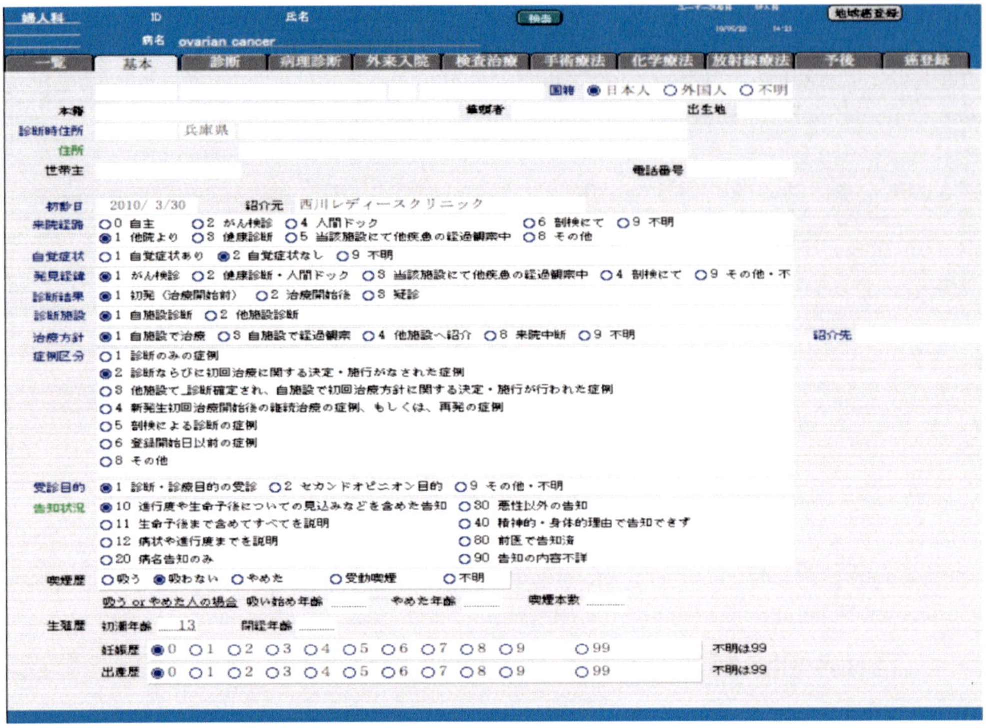

Figure 8: Basic information of cancer patient.

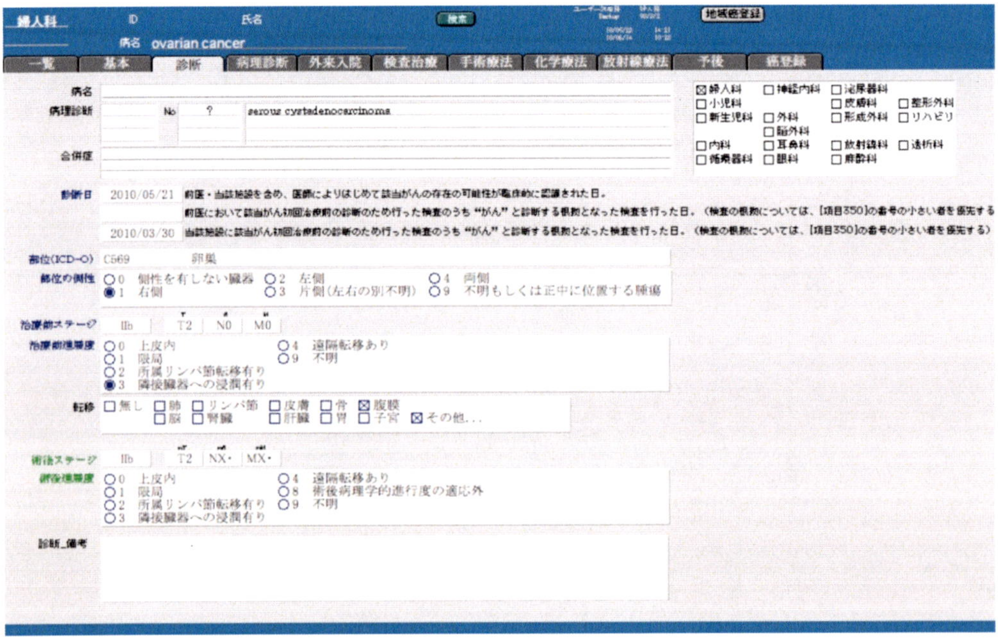

Figure 9: Clinical and pathological diagnostic.

Furthermore, through this record, regimens such as chemotherapy are managed, and treatment plans are also created in this file. Patients' test results can be saved and reviewed as an at-a-glance list or as a graph. The treatment plan can be created while reviewing these results (Figs. **10**, **11**).

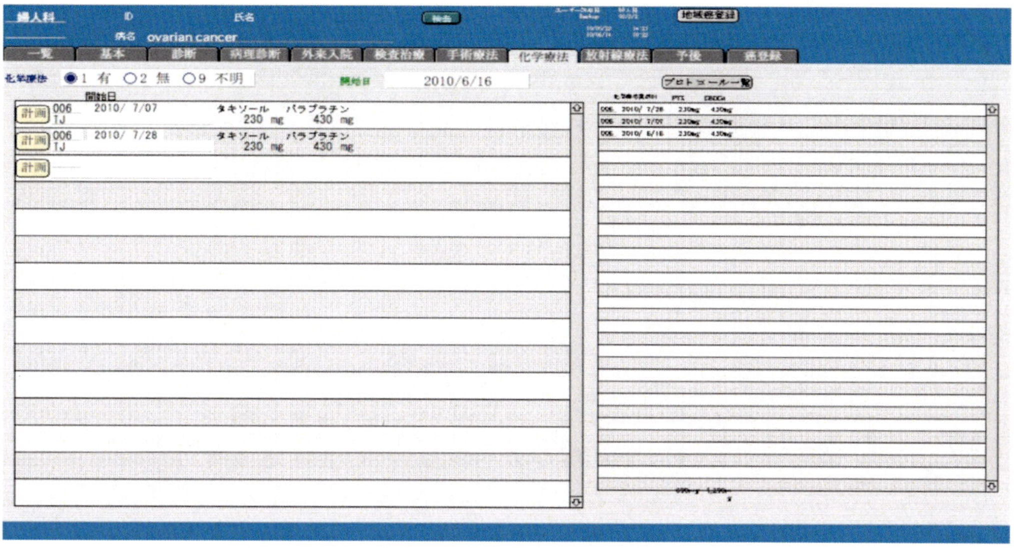

Figure 10: List of chemotherapy history.

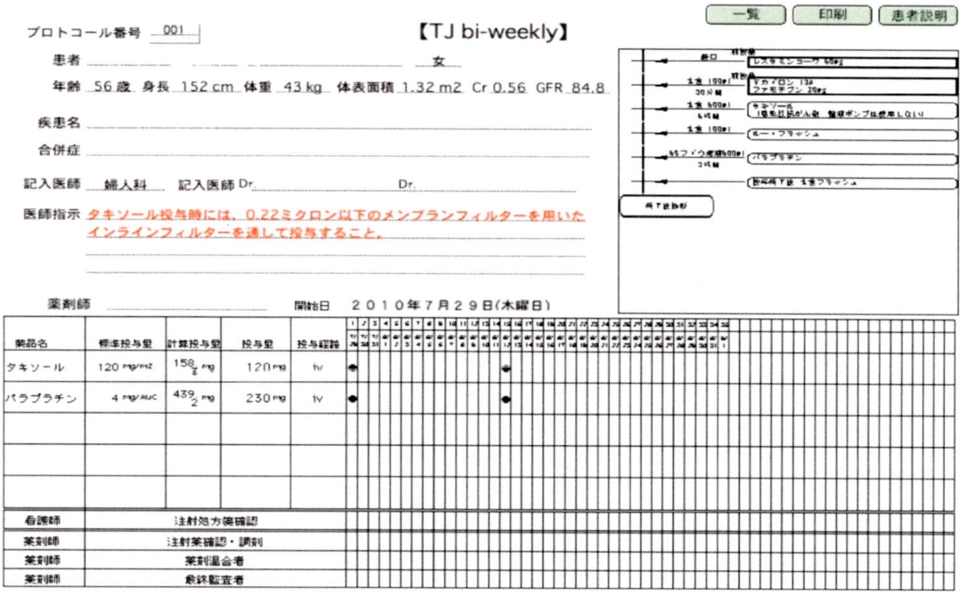

Figure 11: Regimen chart for one course.

4.5. Medical Certificates *etc.*, Creation Support System

The system can create medical and other such certificates by using hospital admission/release information as well as DPC information, *etc.*

In order to claim life insurance benefits, a certificate is necessary. The format is not universal among insurance companies; there are also insurance companies which may have more than ten formats. Furthermore, the certificate must contain detailed information. For this reason, up until now certificates are used to be handwritten. Because it requires so much time and hassle, it has come to be one of a doctor's most hated tasks.

The listed information on the certificate, however, is almost identical to the hospital release summary, and that information may be utilized. This means that if a printer format is created, a certificate can be created just by transferring information from the hospital release summary, DPC information, *etc.* In this system, more than 300 types of print layout are pertaining to individual insurance companies, while sharing and personal information can be transferred from hospital release summaries and DPC information, *etc.* All that then remain to be done is for a doctor or medical secretary to simply review the document, and it can be created. Up until now, it took on average around ten days to issue certificates from the day of request, but this system has made it possible to shorten that time to around four days on average. On top of this, the printout is far more legible than handwritten certificates and mistakes have been minimized (Fig. **12**).

4.6. Pharmacological Management System

The pharmacological management system provides information on drugs to each department. Data is updated as needed, it can be appended with professional comments from the pharmacist, and effects and impacts of drugs can also be searched, making this system a highly useful tool in the clinical sense, too. Furthermore, it is linked with a drug interactions database, so the existence/nonexistence and details of drug interactions may be shown simply by entering multiple names of drugs. An order placement system is also included in this system. By entering the drug code and quantity required, a purchase order is automatically created and divided among different distributors. This process used to require crosschecking records because order amounts to agents were constantly being changed, but there is no longer any need for this. Furthermore, by using stockpiled inventory information, it is possible to manage drug-related finances.

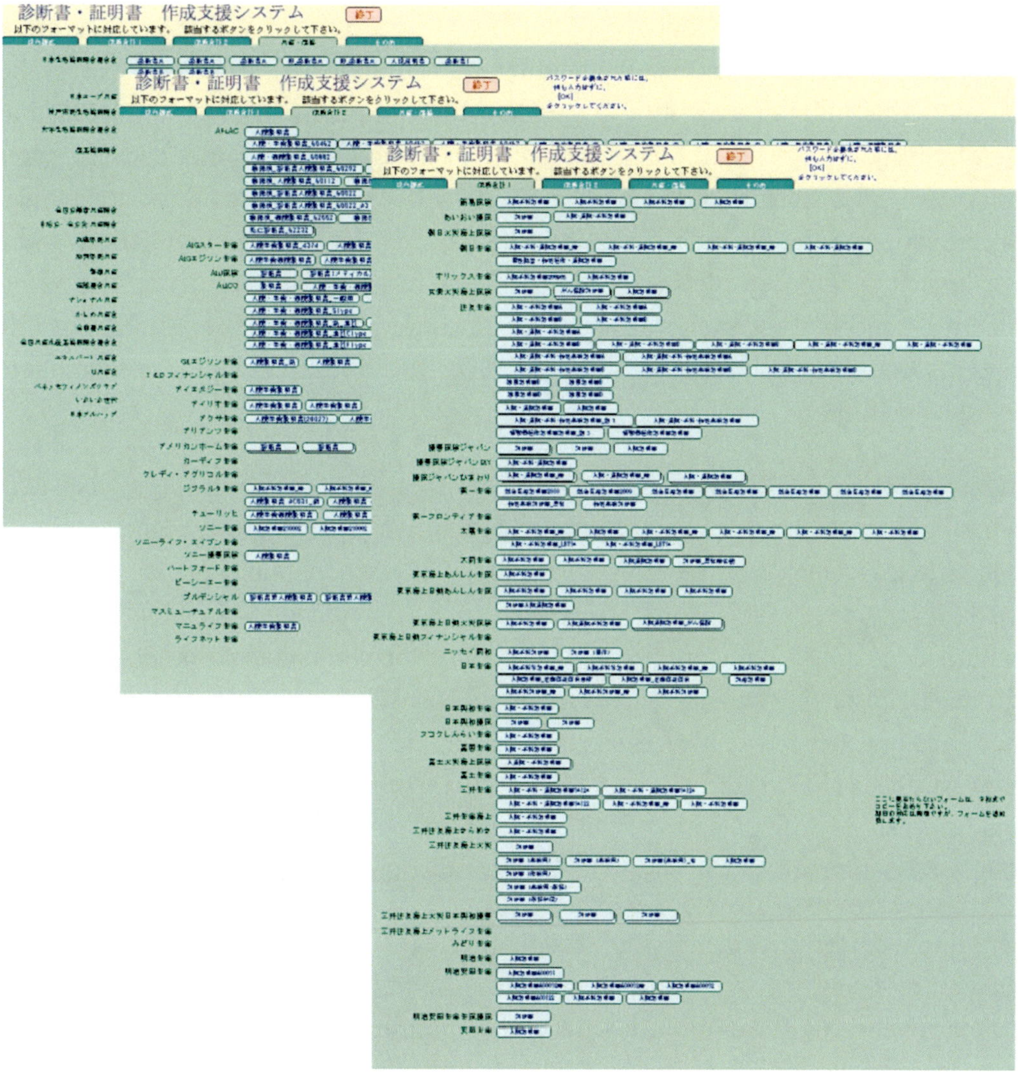

Figure 12: List of medical certifications.

5. WHAT ARE THE ADVANTAGES AND DISADVANTAGES?

The function to create records is a vital part of managing and running a medical facility. The HIS, however, does not possess that function. Furthermore, improving medical transparency and safety requires many documents, but to programme these into the HIS would require extensive labour and time.

If one is dealing with a custom made HIS, adding such functions may be possible, depending on available budget. In recent years packaged software is often adopted, but in these cases, the adding of supplemental functions cannot be performed at individual facilities. To add a function, consent must be obtained at an assembly of users, then taking into account the opinions of other users in order to come to a unanimous agreement; it will take a long time for actual specifications to be decided. Then, it will take even longer for the functions to be implemented. On top of this, HIS has legal restrictions placed upon it as an electronic medical record, and free access to information is not possible. For this reason, the chances of being able to utilize this information for research are extremely slim.

With our original system, the medical professional actually using the system may adjust, change, add, *etc.*, to the system on his/her own. This allows extremely intricate and detailed control and requires a minimum of time to implement. Possibly the greatest advantage of this is that the actual user is able to control the flow of medical information. Information may be organized in their chronological order: outpatient diagnosis, hospital treatment, outpatient follow-ups. Within this flow, information may be added or deleted as needed. Since the user him/herself is able to actually create this flow, she/he is able to create his/her ideal collation of information. Importantly, due to the fact that the accumulation of this information is managed at the tip of the users' fingers, this information can easily be used for other purposes.

On the medical treatment side, hospital release summaries may partially be created by using the information entered in the past and during outpatient visits, which makes this system a powerful tool in both taking a burden off the time of extremely busy medical professionals and in creating accurate release summaries. Furthermore, the system ensures that the reports are chronologically accurate and contain complete data.

Creating medical certificates for insurance companies is one of the most burdensome tasks for doctors: a fact which is confirmed by surveys conducted on the internet telling us of many doctors' extreme dissatisfaction concerning this topic. Many doctors longed for a system which would automatically assist in creating such certificates by using hospital release summaries and DPC information. With the adoption and expansion of this system comes a huge contribution to labour-saving. From surveys I have conducted on the doctors around me, time which used to be spent on making such documents has been saved by an average of one hour per day by these support systems. The system is thus a great help in preventing doctors working too many hours.

On the other hand, original systems have many faults.

It could be argued that, as an ex-programmer who became a doctor, mine is an extremely unique case. Medical professionals are typically not programming experts. Database construction requires a basic pattern of a kind: if the database is not constructed according to this pattern, the system can crash when the database becomes too large. Once it reaches that point, however, reconstructing the database would likely be extremely difficult. It is not realistic to expect medical professionals to learn the basics of database construction. It would probably be necessary for individual facilities to train separate database creators, but in reality this would probably prove difficult. Thus, the system must be created following basic minimum rules.

Specifically, looking at the programming content itself raises various problems. Protocol problems include no consistency in the nomenclature of field and script, *etc.,* and serviceability being extremely bad due to a lack of comments. A record of modifications to the system is not kept; the steps to prevent the possibility of bugs embedded in the system are not undertaken; *etc.,* Many of these types of problems arise in programming.

The untested nature of the program is another problem which may become a bug in itself. Problems arise such as the possibility of when setting conditions, the hypothesized value of conditions may be underestimated; or, if an error were to occur, there is no way of dealing with it. If the system were something that the programmer him/herself were to use privately, she/he could immediately cope with and correct the problem on site, but when it is an enormous database which is involved in day-to-day work, it may cause business to be suspended. In order to solve these problems, I believe that educating programmers at the foundation level using training courses, *etc.*, is invaluable.

Next, the person in charge of the system may be transferred to another location for work. If the person in charge is unavailable, manufactured systems have documents prepared so that the successor may carry on the system maintenance. Original systems, however, do not have such documents, and algorithmic problems make it very hard for others other than the creator of the system to perform maintenance. Also, copyright issues can make it impossible for the creator to use the system at his/her new place of work.

Original systems may indeed harbor many problems, but they also have many more great advantages which far outnumber these issues. These systems are a means by which medical professionals can organize their own work.

File-maker is very flexible database software which even a beginner can master. I believe this is the optimum tool for a user himself/herself, according to his/her level, to collect and process many different types of information. It is also completely original in its allowing the user to modify its construction even while operating it. therefore, everyone, won't you follow us and try making your own systems?

CONFLICT OF INTEREST

None declared.

ACKNOWLEDGEMENT

None declared.

REFERENCES

[1] FileMaker, Inc., http://www.filemaker.co.jp/ (2010.8.12).
[2] Fujitsu Ltd., http://jp.fujitsu.com/solutions/medical/products/egmainfx/ (2010.8.12).
[3] KEY Planning.co.,ltd., http://www.key-planning.co.jp/ (2010.8.12).
[4] Rolan, inc., http://www.rolan.co.jp/shouhin/sqr_plus.html (2010.8.12).

CHAPTER 9

Small System Suitable For Team Working With Diabetes Mellitus Patients

Tatsuhiko Koga[1,*] and Hiroshi Hara[2]

[1]Haradoi Hospital, 6-40-8 Aoba, Higashi-Ku, Fukuoka, Japan and [2]Haradoi Hospital, 6-40-8 Aoba, Higashi-Ku, Fukuoka, Japan

Abstract: Over the last 20 years, we have developed a small database system using FileMaker Pro to follow patients with diabetes mellitus. We developed this system because there were no electric database systems available at Yamaguchi Red Cross Hospital in 1989. Most hospitals now have Electronic Health Record (EHR) systems. However, these systems were developed for common clinical usage, and do not track sufficient specialised information to allow us to follow a particular disease. Therefore, small systems in addition to EHR are still required. Medical staff usually do not have sufficient computer skills to develop and maintain such systems, but generally have adequate skills to use these systems as well as the desire to maintain the health of their patients. It is important for medical staff to learn to make databases themselves to be able to obtain sufficient information regarding their patients while maintaining sufficient levels of privacy.

Keywords: SDM, diabetes mellituS, FileMaker Pro, team work, complications, home doctor, medical information letter, medical manuals, Cancer, XML.

1. INTRODUCTION

On returning to Japan in 1989 after a 2-year stay as a postdoctoral fellow at Johns Hopkins University in Baltimore, Maryland, USA, I took up a position at Yamaguchi Red Cross Hospital as a medical doctor, mainly for patients suffering from diabetes mellitus. Several months later, I decided to make a database to follow these patients for several reasons. The reason for selecting a computer system will be discussed in addition to the clinical considerations.

On first arriving at Johns Hopkins in 1987, I was told that former researchers from Japan worked hard but often did not leave sufficient documentation of their

***Address correspondence to Tatsuhiko Koga:** Department of Internal Medicine, Haradoi Hospital, Japan; E-mail: tatskoga@qf6.so-net.ne.jp experiments. On the same day, I purchased an Apple IIc computer to create and store all records on floppy disks. The Apple IIc was newer than the previous generation Apple IIe, had 128 kB of memory and was portable. I had a monitor in my lab and another at home and carried the computer to the two locations every day. After two years of study, it became obvious that, if correctly input, the computer could be a powerful tool for maintaining medical records.

Later, I purchased a liquid crystal display and heavy batteries and expanded the memory to 1024 kB to operate GEOS OS, which was a Macintosh-like operation system for Apple II that used a mouse. The clock speed of the IIc was only 1 MHz, and so the operating speed was slow despite the expanded memory. In addition, the IIc was an 8-bit computer and so could not work with 2-byte code, such as the Japanese language. Nevertheless, GeoWord (word processor), GeoCalc (spreadsheet) and GeoFiles (database) software were attractive applications for the GEOS OS platform. Several months prior to leaving Baltimore, I purchased a Macintosh SE/30 with 1 MB of memory and 40MB Hard Disk Drive, as well as Sweet-Jam, which was a module to allow use of the Japanese language in Microsoft Word and Excel on System 6.0.3 (English OS).

2. MULTIPLE STEPS FOR EXPANSION FROM A SYSTEM WITH NO ELECTRIC HOSPITAL RECORDS

2.1. First Step for Clinical Support of Diabetic Patients

At Yamaguchi Red Cross Hospital, I saw more than 20 outpatients every day at the diabetes clinic. The clinical aim was not only to control blood glucose level but also to prevent the advance of diabetes complications, neuropathy, retinopathy, nephropathy heart disease and cerebral vascular disease. I could not memorise the stage of every complication of a diabetic patient, but I had to finish all tasks for one outpatient within ten minutes at least.

There were no Electronic Health Record (EHR) systems at Yamaguchi Red Cross Hospital in 1989, so I had to make the necessary tools myself.

I felt that it was necessary to display important information in a single layout and to include several buttons for prescriptions, blood examinations and a field for clinical history. I began to build a database with GeoFile on Apple IIc, but it took a lot of time to extract suitable information from this system. Then, I found FileMaker Pro 2.1, which was similar in operation to GeoFiles but had excellent speed, and it ran in 32-bit native mode on the Apple Macintosh SE/30.

A computerised database for the medical records of diabetic patients was necessary as several patients were also found to have malignant disease and it was not possible to memorise every date and the results of chest X-ray examination, upper GI examination, ultrasound examination, *etc.*, for these cases. Therefore, I prepared twelve fields in the database to find early cancer in the diabetes clinic (Fig. **1**).

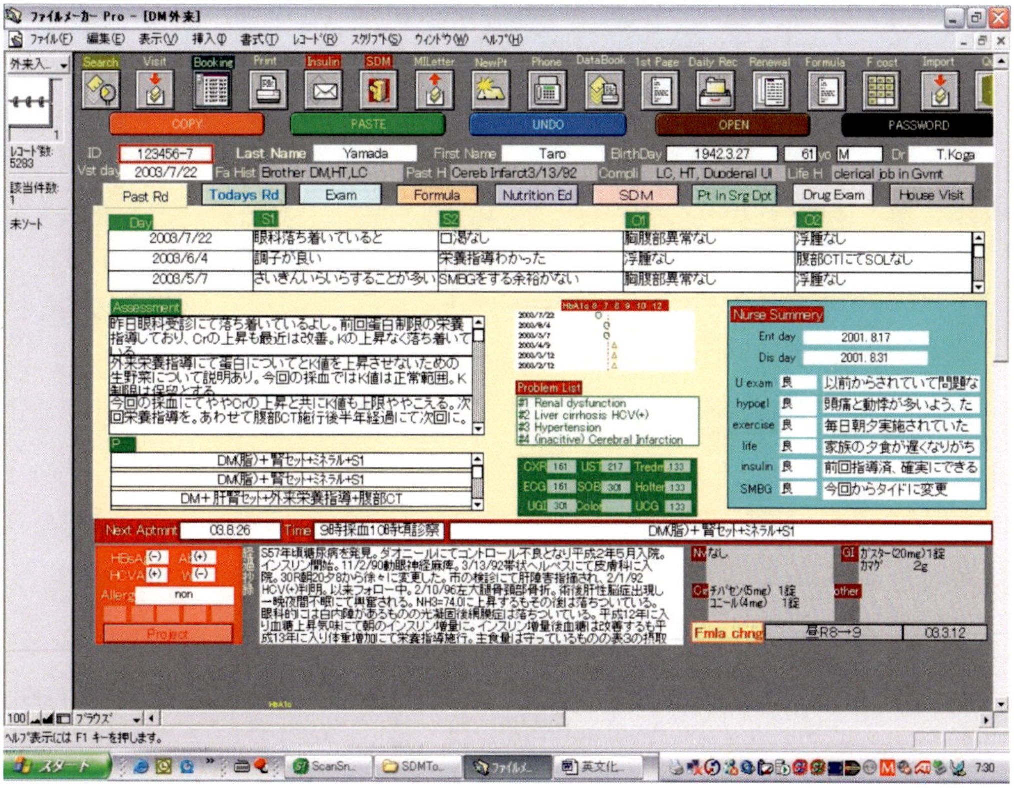

Figure 1: The start menu of this system partially translated into English for presentation at the International Diabetes Congress held in Paris in 2003.

2.2. Second Step for Saving Daily Records

FileMaker was updated to v3.0 in 1995, and included relational database capabilities. Therefore, I prepared two additional files: the "ID file" was related *via* the ID number and had ten fields (ID number, name, address, social status, date of birth, *etc.,*) with a different password for security; and "daily record", which had eight fields (ID number, date, subjective 1, subjective 2, objective 1, objective 2, assessment and plan). This change allowed all records to be stored on computer suing FileMaker without any need for paper copies.

Several related files could be completed *via* a single layout by clicking on the popup menu (Fig. **2**).

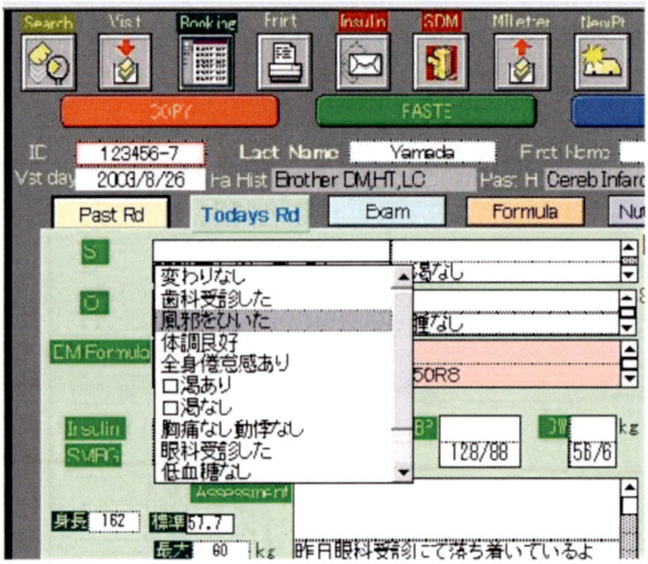

Figure 2: Popup menu for input dairy record.

After completing each field, click the "Print" button, and a prescription sheet (left side), medical record portion (upper right portion), which should be pasted onto paper after signing and the next appointment sheet (lower right portion) will be printed on A4 paper (Fig. **3**)

The database files were used to produce medical information letters (Fig. **4**) toward physicians who referred diabetic patients to Yamaguchi Red Cross Hospital not only for the Department of Internal Medicine but also for the Department of Surgery to undergo various operations at discharge hospital.

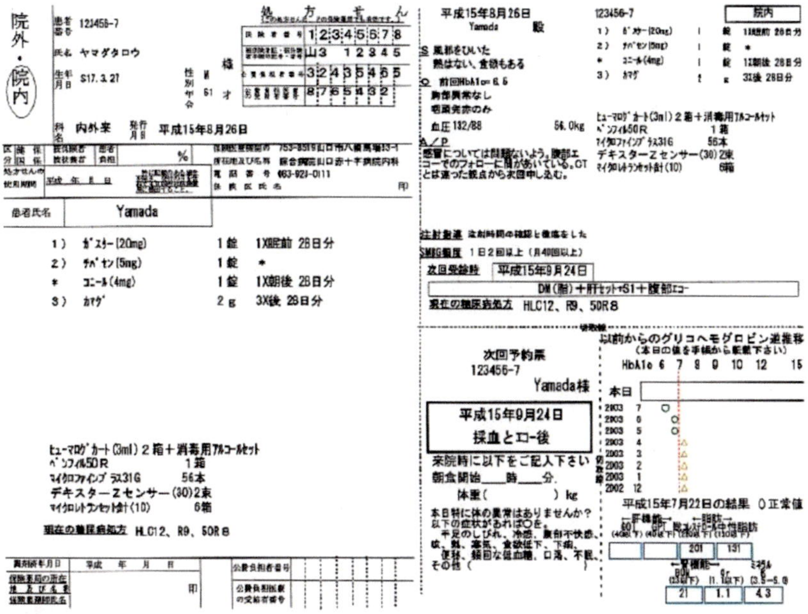

平成15年8月26日

Yamada

1） ｶﾞｽﾀｰ(20mg) 1錠 1X眠前 28日分
2） ﾁﾊﾞｾﾝ(5mg) 1錠 〃
〃 ｺﾆｰﾙ(4mg) 1錠 1X朝後 28日分
3） ｶﾏｸﾞ 2g 3X後 28日分

ﾋｭｰﾏﾛｸﾞｶｰﾄ(3ml) 2箱＋消毒用ｱﾙｺｰﾙｾｯﾄ
ﾍﾟﾝﾌｨﾙ50R 1箱
ﾏｲｸﾛﾌｧｲﾝﾌﾟﾗｽ31G 56本
デキスターＺセンサー(30) 2束
ﾏｲｸﾛﾚｯﾄﾗﾝｾｯﾄ針(10) 6箱

現在の糖尿病処方 HLC12、R9、50R8

次回予約票
123456-7
Yamada様
平成15年9月24日
採血とエコー後

Figure 3: A-4 printout for outpatient.

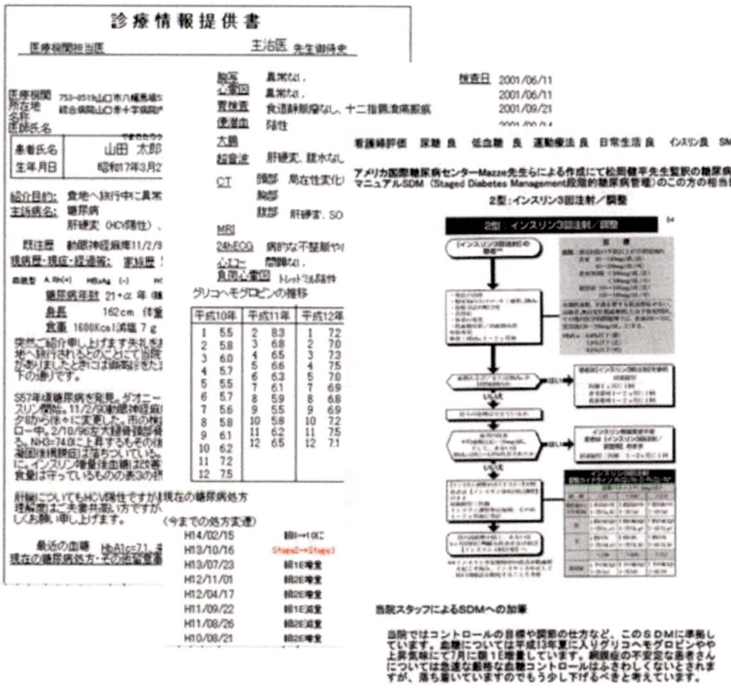

診療情報提供書

Figure 4: Medical information sheets made at hospital discharge.

The first page was composed of the medical history, the second was automatically filled with examination data, and the third page contained prospective proposals for future treatment according to the Staged Diabetes Management (SDM) manual along with our comments.

The SDM (Staged Diabetes Management) was originally made by the Internal Diabetes Center in Minneapolis, MN, USA in 1985 for home doctors who were non-specialists in diabetes mellitus [1], and was customised by Dr. Kempei Matsuoka and the SDM Study Group, Japan [2]. It has a two-page manual for each stage of diabetes mellitus, and the patient file was linked to the SDM manual with every stage

The related comments of the SDM manual are shown by clicking the 6th tab. Other pages can be selected by clicking the SDM stage popup menu (Fig. **5**).

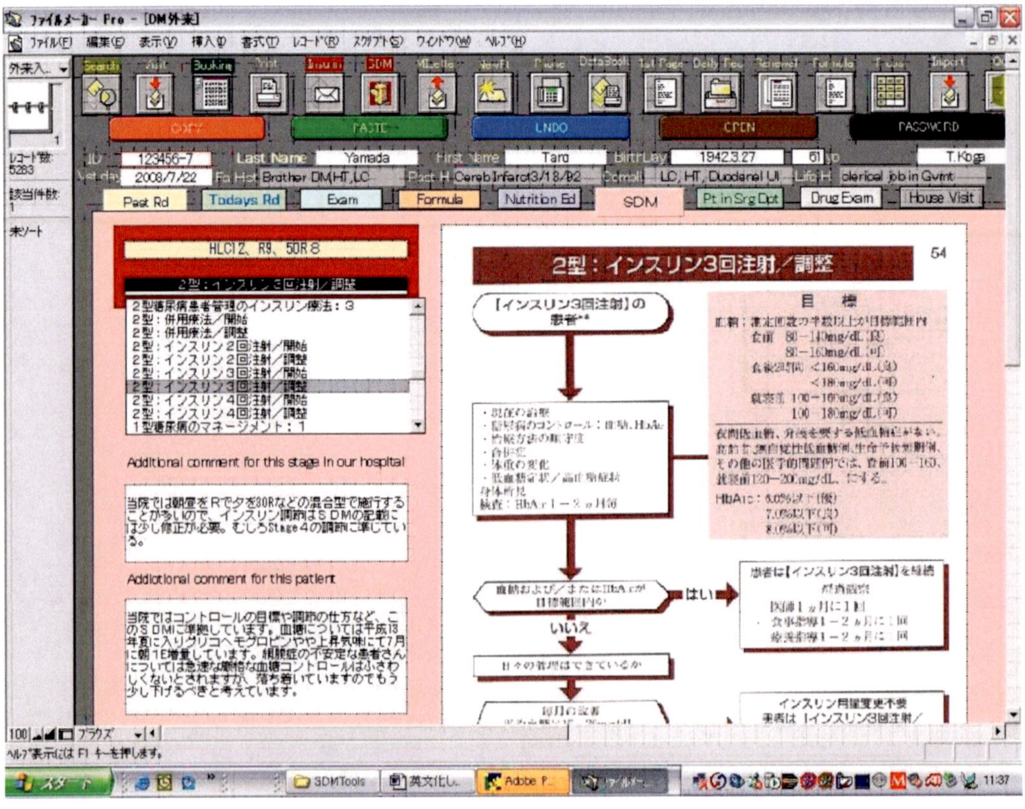

Figure 5: SDM manual description.

2.3. Third Step for Group Work with Co-Medical Staff

Medication itself is not the only form of treatment for diabetic patients. For example, with the aid of a dietician, patients must learn how to calculate food balance. In addition, consultations with nurses and medical trainers are required to determine a suitable lifestyle and exercise regime. Several relational files were added to the database for co-medical staff to share selected medical information to facilitate patient education. There was no network in the hospital, so the information in several relational files was updated every other day.

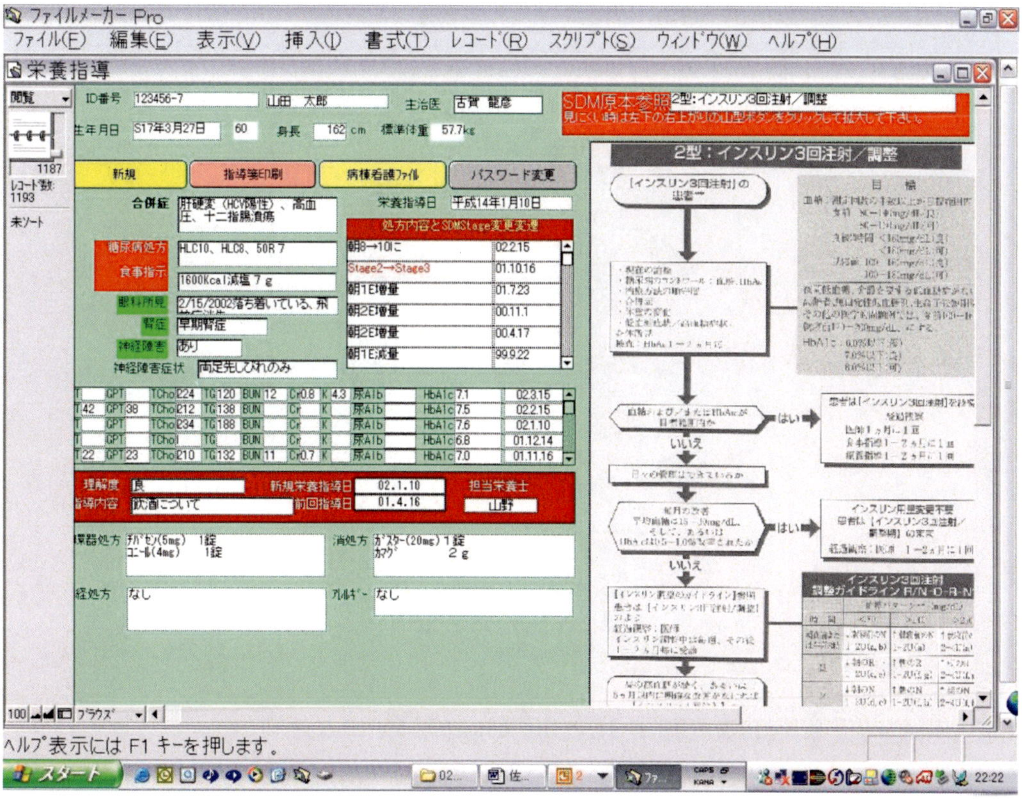

Figure 6: Start menu for dietitian.

Two relational files were added to hold the results of blood examinations. These files had about 50 fields, including ID number, blood glucose, HbA1c, AST, ALT, UN, Cr, *etc.* The medical technicians in the hospital laboratory were asked to transfer all blood data into CSV files every day, which were then imported into FileMaker relational files every day. Thus, it became possible for us to obtain lab data without the risk of errors introduced by typing. Clerks were also asked to transfer date records of patients to the Division of Ophthalmology every day, and we could see the date of the last visiting for all patients automatically from the relational database using the ID number as a key.

This view shows the condition of the patient (Fig. **6**). Co-workers can also refer to the SDM page. Fig. **7** shows a sample report made by a dietician as a record of a 10-min consultation.

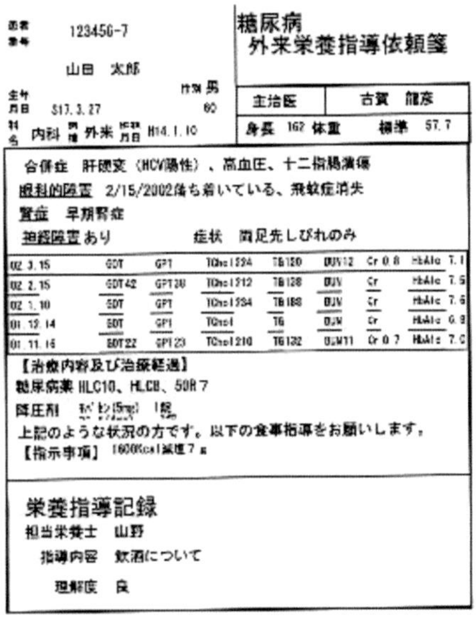

糖尿病
外来栄養指導依頼箋

患者番号 123456-7
山田 太郎
性別 男
生年月日 S17.3.27 60
科名 内科 病棟 外来 依頼月日 H14.1.10
主治医 古賀 龍彦
身長 167 体重 標準 57.7

合併症 肝硬変（HCV陽性）、高血圧、十二指腸潰瘍
眼科的障害 2/15/2002落ち着いている、飛蚊症消失
腎症 早期腎症
神経障害あり 症状 両足先しびれのみ

02.3.15	GOT	GPT	TChol 224	TG 120	BUN 12	Cr 0.8	HbA1c	7.1
02.2.15	GOT 42	GPT 20	TChol 212	TG 128	BUN	Cr	HbA1c	7.5
02.1.10	GOT	GPT	TChol 234	TG 188	BUN	Cr	HbA1c	7.6
01.12.14	GOT	GPT	TChol	TG	BUN	Cr	HbA1c	6.9
01.11.16	GOT 22	GPT 23	TChol 210	TG 132	BUN 11	Cr 0.7	HbA1c	7.0

【治療内容及び治療経過】
糖尿病薬 HLC10、HLC8、50R7
降圧剤 [illegible](5mg) 1錠
上記のような状況の方です。以下の食事指導をお願いします。
【指示事項】 1600Kcal 塩種7g

栄養指導記録
担当栄養士 山野
指導内容 飲酒について
理解度 良

Figure 7: Report sheet made by dietician.

2.4. Trial for Patients to Show Insulin Algorithm

To prevent hypoglycaemia, young patients are taught how to manage their insulin dose. Insulin adjustment guidelines were displayed in the database by adding a new layout (Fig. **8**).

The explanation letter (Fig. **9**) suitable for this stage was printed by clicking the button to select stage (Fig. **8**). As it was sometimes difficult for elderly patients to understand and the trial was stressful for these subjects, the trial was continued only in selected patients.

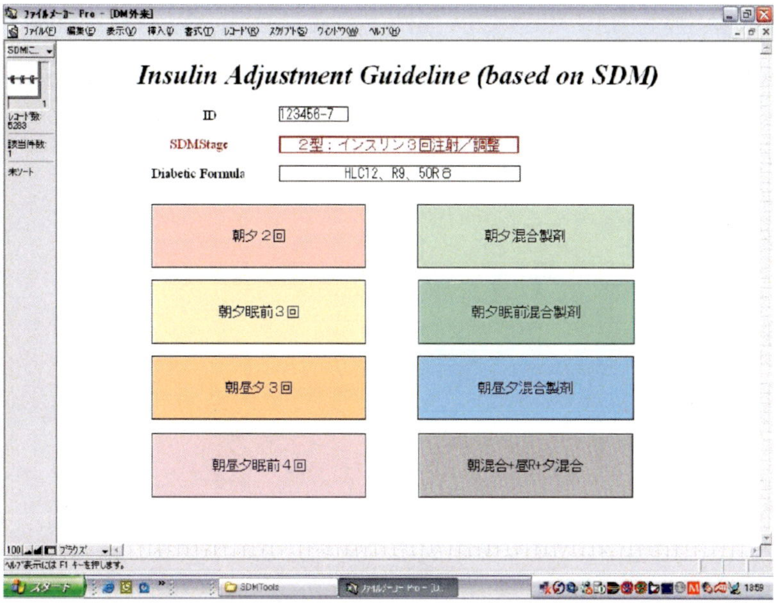

Figure 8: Buttons for printing insulin algorithm.

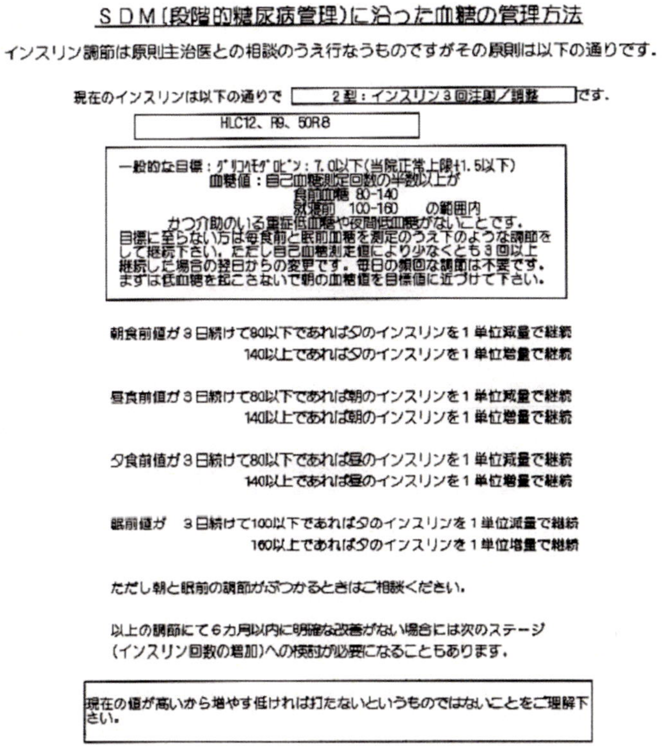

SＤＭ(段階的糖尿病管理)に沿った血糖の管理方法

インスリン調節は原則主治医との相談のうえ行なうものですがその原則は以下の通りです。

現在のインスリンは以下の通りで［２型：インスリン３回注射／調整］です。

［HLC12、R9、50R8］

一般的な目標：グリコヘモグロビン：7.0以下(当院正常上限+1.5以下)
血糖値：自己血糖測定回数の半数以上が
食前血糖 80-140
就寝前 100-160 の範囲内
かつ介助のいる重症低血糖や夜間低血糖がないことです。
目標に至らない方は毎食前と眠前血糖を測定のうえ下のような調節をして継続下さい。ただし自己血糖測定値により少なくとも３回以上継続した場合の翌日からの変更です。毎日の頻回な調節は不要です。
まずは低血糖を起こさないで朝の血糖値を目標値に近づけて下さい。

朝食前値が３日続けて80以下であれば夕のインスリンを１単位減量で継続
140以上であれば夕のインスリンを１単位増量で継続

昼食前値が３日続けて80以下であれば朝のインスリンを１単位減量で継続
140以上であれば朝のインスリンを１単位増量で継続

夕食前値が３日続けて80以下であれば昼のインスリンを１単位減量で継続
140以上であれば昼のインスリンを１単位増量で継続

眠前値が　３日続けて100以下であれば夕のインスリンを１単位減量で継続
160以上であれば夕のインスリンを１単位増量で継続

ただし朝と眠前の調節がぶつかるときはご相談ください。

以上の調節にて６カ月以内に明確な改善がない場合には次のステージ(インスリン回数の増加)への検討が必要になることもあります。

現在の値が高いから増やす低ければ打たないというものではないことをご理解下さい。

Figure 9: Printout regarding insulin adjustment.

2.5. Manual for Pre- and Post-Operative Control of Blood Glucose

It is necessary to control the blood glucose levels of inpatients awaiting surgical procedures. I prepared several patterns for this purpose, which provided good support (Fig. **10**).

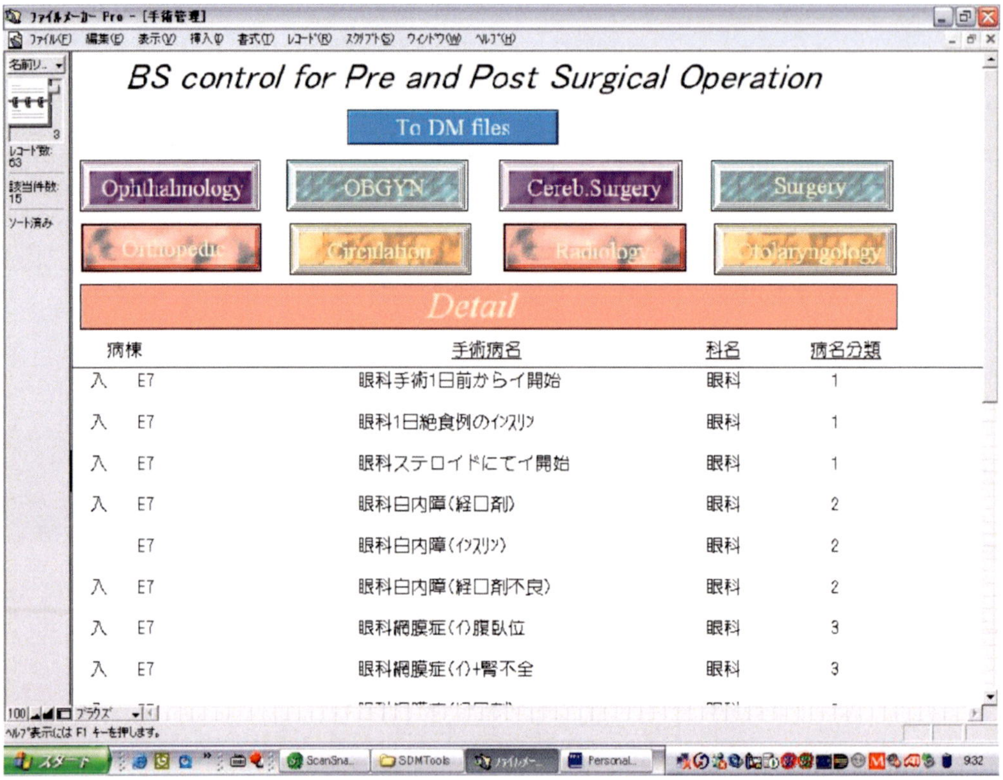

Figure 10: Button to select operation type.

2.6. Data Export by FileMaker v6

An XML export function was added to FileMaker in v6. To exchange data with other hospitals, this function was used to export data into XML format, which was the format recommended by the Japanese Association for Medical Informatics (JAMI) (Fig. **11**).

FileMaker v6 also included PDA connectivity with FileMaker Mobile 2.1. It was possible to exchange data from 20 fields, and it was very convenient to be able to carry current data to the patients' bedsides.

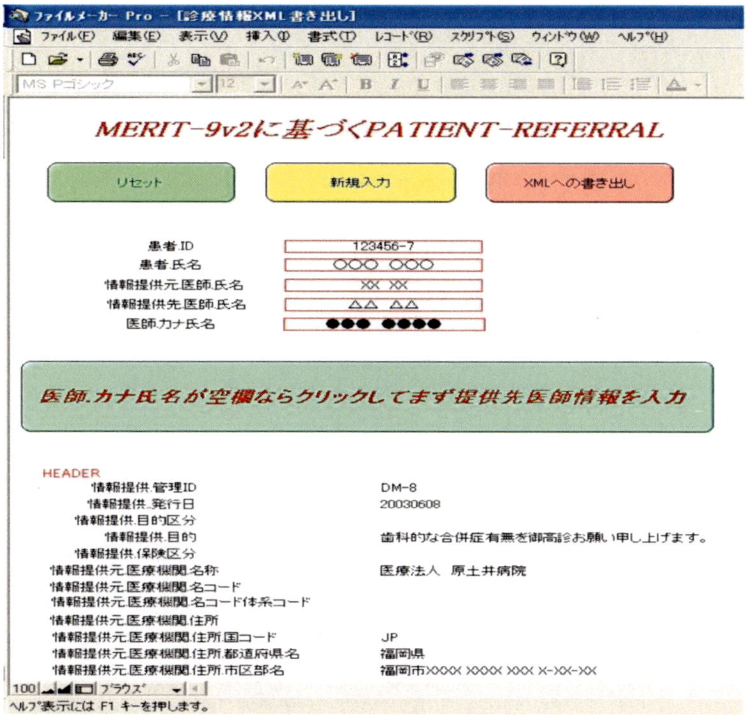

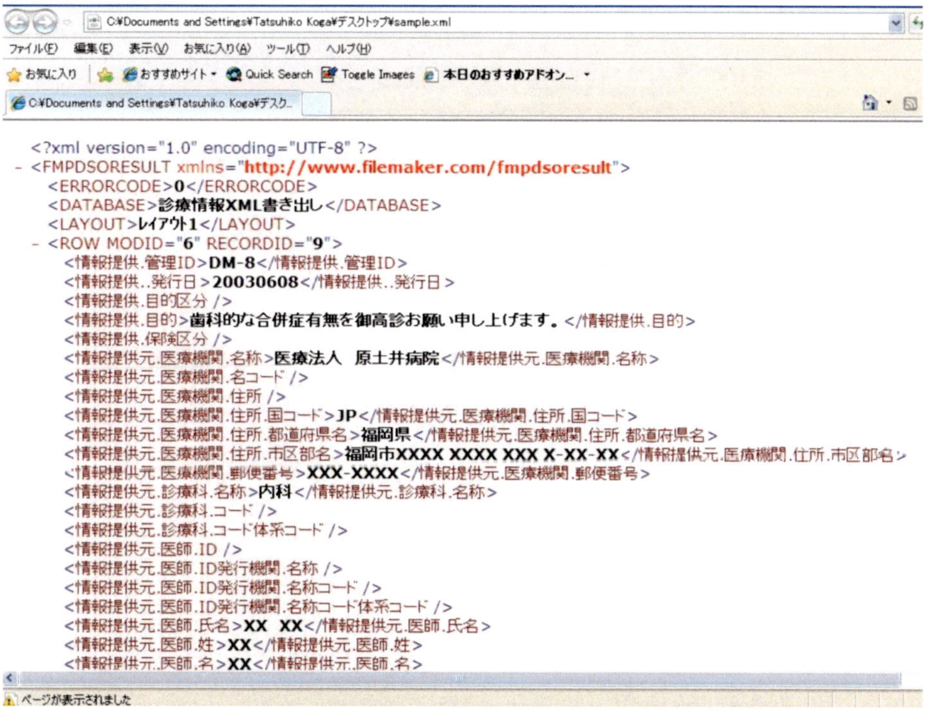

Figure 11: Export data into XML format.

3. FURTHER STEP FOR EXPAND WITH COMMON ELECTRIC HOSPITAL RECORD SYSTEM

Before leaving Yamaguchi Red Cross Hospital in 2003, I handed over the diabetes-specific system to younger staff, and then began working at HaraDoi Hospital in Fukuoka City. In this hospital, an Electronic Health Record (EHR) system was under construction, and I became a member of the committee to implement this system.

I initially imagined that it would be possible to expand the same concepts as used in Yamaguchi Red Hospital, but it soon became clear that the type of this huge system was completely different from the system developed previously. The EHR had to be operated by many kinds of doctors with varied specialties; dermatologists did not necessarily need to know the level of HbA1c, but this represented important information for doctors engaged in care of patients with diabetes mellitus.

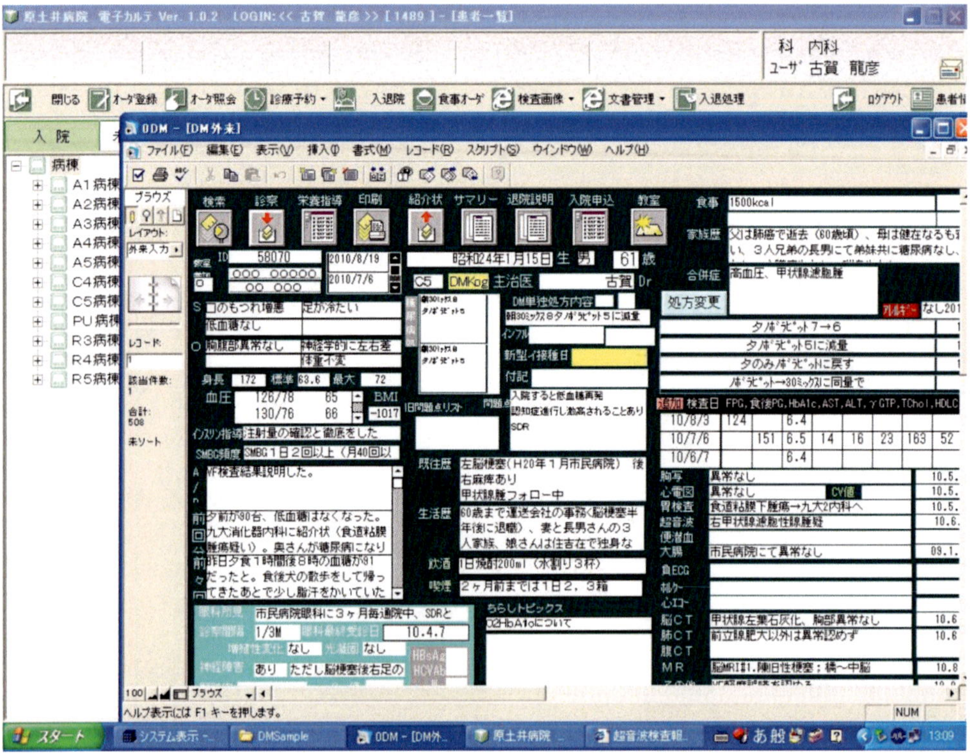

Figure 12: Cooperation of EHR and FileMaker file for diabetes.

I again began to use a small system for diabetes developed in FileMaker v7, and later began to use this system on another computer unrelated to the EHR to prevent the possibility of problems with the EHR. Later, I used FileMaker Pro Advanced to develop a standalone file to be operated on terminal computers of the EHR without installation of FileMaker Pro [3], and could operate EHR and FileMaker Files in the same screen (Fig. **12**).

To provide patients with a DM note that keeps track of data, body weight and blood pressure on every visit, I added a suitable layout to print the data with information selected from more than sixty titles using popup menus (Fig. **13**).

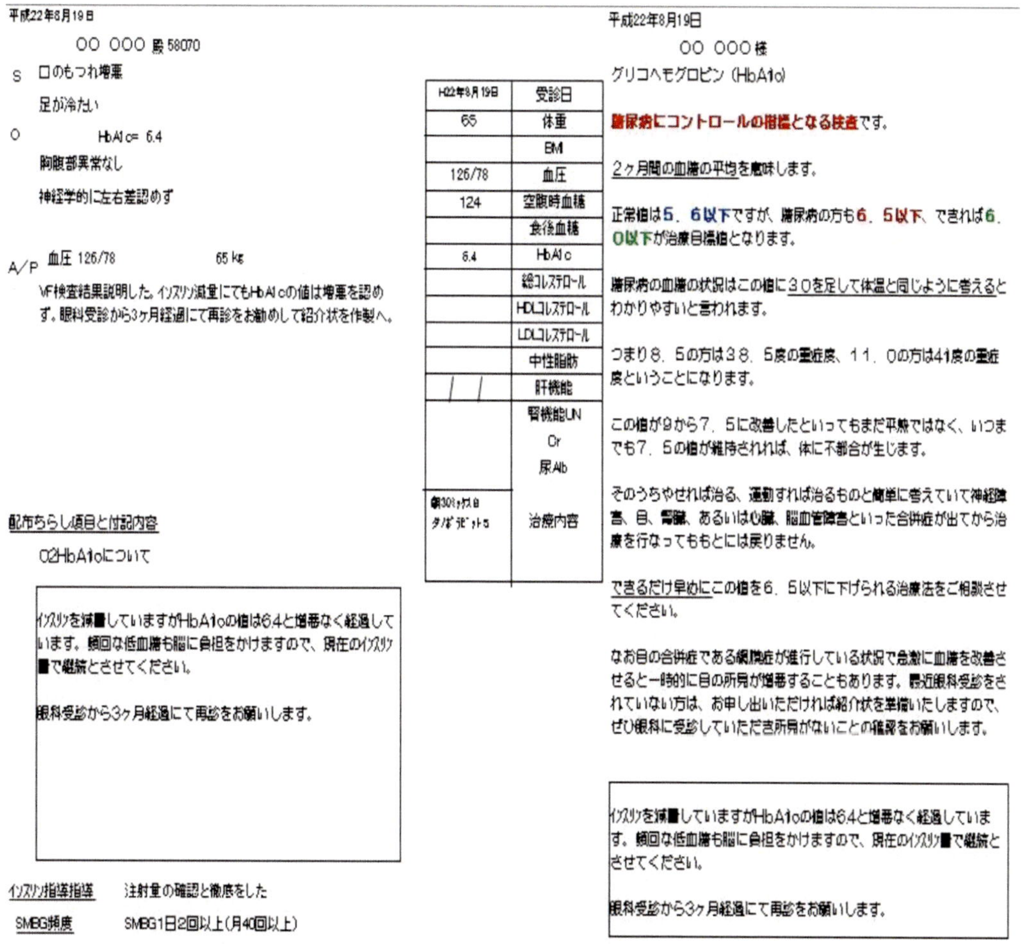

Figure 13: A4 sheet printed out for every outpatient. Left, medical record; center, DM note; right, patient education. This sample refer to the significance of HbA1c.

I also added a layout for inpatients to describe daily records (Fig. **14**).

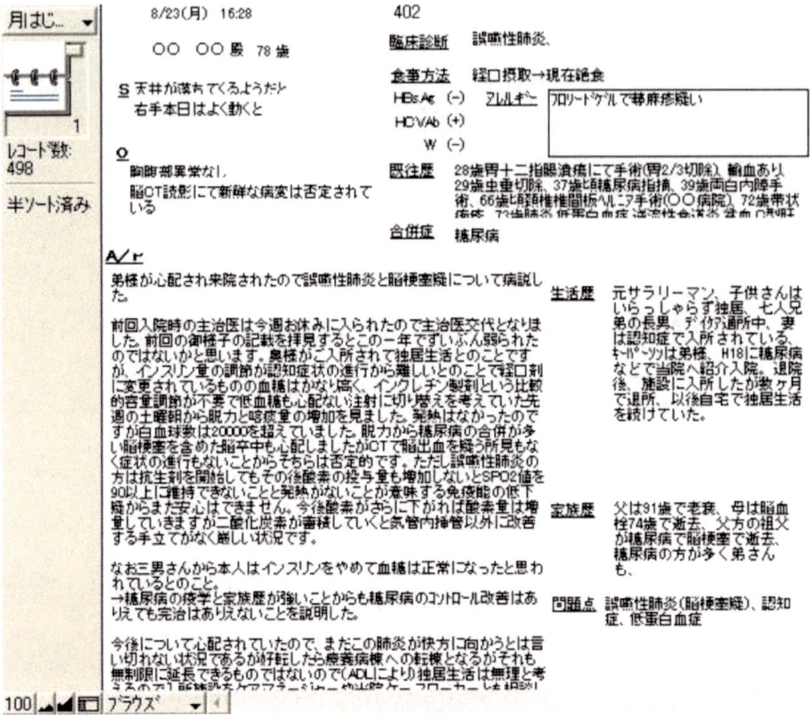

Figure 14: Layout for inpatient daily record.

4. DISCUSSIONS

The system described here was developed with the aim of gaining better insight into clinical management of diabetic patients. Changing to the new working environment at HaraDoi Hospital, in which a new EHR was being deployed, was an important experience, and I came to realise that EHR could not support all requirements in various clinical situations. EHR can simplify common tasks. However, to satisfy clinical needs, it is usually necessary for physicians to develop additional databases ourselves to save additional cost.

It was lucky that I encountered the easy to use FileMaker database software. It was also fortunate that FileMaker was originally a simple, easy to learn card-type database and that it developed into a relational database gradually. FileMaker is sufficiently simple for medical doctors to learn on their own and suitable layouts can be added as necessary.

One of the most important problems associated with the use of FileMaker in clinical situations is its simple structure. It is necessary to maintain patient privacy, and we must avoid leakage of data. Many hospitals have tried to use high-security EHR systems as gateways for FileMaker files in various ways. We need to exchange each trial to succeed. I am going to use an additional function of FileMaker, web-share function to hide database files and avoid to carry it out. I would like to report the advanced results later.

CONFLICT OF INTEREST

None declared.

ACKWOWLEDGEMENTS

This system was presented at the International Diabetes Congress held in Paris in 2003 and 28th Joint Conference on Medical Informatics 2008 in Japan. The authors are grateful to the researchers present at these conferences for their comments. The authors are also grateful to the co-workers for advice at Yamaguchi Red Cross Hospital and at Hara-Doi Hospital.

REFERENCES

[1] Mazze, R, Strock, E., Etzwiler, D, Staged Diabetes Management Decision Path. International Diabetes Center, Minneapolis, 1995.
[2] Matsuoka, K, Staged Diabetes Management 2008, SDM Meeting Tokyo, 2008.
[3] Koga, T, A sub-database system for the specific following of diabetic patients. Obesity and Diabetes 2009 (supple8): 62-66.

CHAPTER 10

Improvement of Workflows in Health Screening For Employees by Making Use of Existing Systems and FileMaker Pro

Shunji Wakamiya[1,*] and Kazunobu Yamauchi[2]

[1]Kawasaki Medical School, 577 Matsushima, Kurashiki, Okamaya, Japan and [2]Fujita Health University, 1-98 Dengakugakubo, Kutsukake, Toyoake, Aichi, Japan

Abstract: Here, we report a new approach to the systematization of health screening for employees at a hospital that involves developing a new system requiring little capital investment. A new system was developed with FileMaker Pro using existing order entry and radiological health screening systems. The effectiveness of this new system was examined by comparing the implementation efficiency of health screening for employees before and after its introduction, and by comparison with another such system currently in place at other medical institutions with regard to efficiency. Although the new system has been in place for more than three years, no problems have yet been encountered. This new system is very useful in this hospital and may also be useful for institutions where it is difficult to introduce expensive new systems for systematic health screening because of problems regarding capital management.

Keywords: Health screening, employee, order entry, radiography, FileMaker Pro, workflows, existing systems, systematization, hospital, capital management.

1. INTRODUCTION

Health screening for employees (HSE) is implemented regularly at both hospitals and other types of institution to improve and maintain health care in accordance with Japan's Industrial Safety and Health Law. Although HSE is consigned to a hospital at non-medical institutions, it is ordinarily implemented *in situ* at hospitals themselves. However, the workloads of both employees undergoing checkups and of staff performing these checkups are lower at large hospitals, which have many full-time staff and where patient and staff health care are independent of each other, than at smaller hospitals where HSE is implemented in addition to the staffs' normal daily work in patient care. Many commercial

***Address correspondence to Shunji Wakamiya:** Department of Ophthalmology, Kawasaki Medical School, Japan; E-mail: oph@mtj.biglobe.ne.jp

systems for health screening of patients are available in Japan [1-9]. Despite their frequent use as health screening systems for employees as well as for patients at larger hospitals, these systems have seldom been introduced at smaller hospitals.

This may be because smaller hospitals cannot make the necessary financial investment in health screening systems for employees.

Implementation of HSE can be highly complex, as screening schedules differ according to employee's age, occupational category, and the season in which HSE is implemented, and as the HSE workflow includes many steps: decision and notification of screening schedules and dates for each employee, ordering of physical examinations, such as blood and/or urine sample collection, transcription of results to screening reports, transcription of results of internal medical examinations, and final notification of HSE results to each employee, *etc.* When this is done manually, it is clear that the workload of the staff in charge and the difficulty in determining how many employees must have checkups are proportional to the total number of employees at the institution.

Therefore, we developed a new low-cost system for HSE using existing systems at a general hospital. In this paper, we discuss the significance and benefits of our system in comparison with another such system currently in place at other medical institutions.

2. METHODS

A new system was introduced in 2004 at Hamamatsu Rosai Hospital (HR), which has 21 departments, 400 beds (350 beds at present), and about 500 staff, and is one of the hospitals founded for workers' health by Labor Welfare Corporation under the control of the Ministry of Labor (currently, the Ministry of Health, Labor, and Welfare) of Japan.

2.1. Hardware and Software

Three existing systems were used to develop a new health screening system for employees: a standalone radiological health screening system (Easy-2001;

Landauer Inc., Glenwood, IL), an order entry system (EGMAIN; Fujitsu, Kawasaki, Japan) incorporated into a 100BASE-T/10BASE-T Ethernet network, which collaborated with a clinical laboratory system, and an ophthalmologic support system the server for which was embedded in an order entry system network The ophthalmologic support system, which was developed by one of the authors (S.W.) with FileMaker Pro 5.0 and FileMaker Server 5.0, utilized the terminal clients of the order entry system and its own server.

The operating systems used were Windows NT 4.0 Workstation for order entry system clients and Windows 2000 Professional for the radiological health screening system and the server of the ophthalmologic support system.

Customization to process data from the order entry system to diskette in CSV format was consigned to the vendor developing the order entry system. Data from the radiological screening system were exported to diskette in CSV format using the standard system menu. A new health screening system for employees was developed with FileMaker Pro 5.0 (Japanese Edition) and was designed to import data from diskette in CSV format. The functions of the new system, such as importing data and printing the final results, were implemented with scripts using standard functions of FileMaker Pro. Four new files were made with FileMaker Pro: a file for employee information (A), a file for importing data from the order entry system (B), a file for importing data from the radiological health screening system (C), and a file for examination data (D). FileMaker Pro 5.0 was installed in one of the order entry system clients where these four files were used.

Figs. **1-4** show the start menus of this new system included in the file for examination data (D), the file for importing data from the order entry system (B), the file for importing data from the radiological health screening system (C), and the file for employee information (A). These four files were managed with FileMaker Server 5.0 installed on the server of the ophthalmologic support system. These files were backed up using one of the management functions of FileMaker Server.

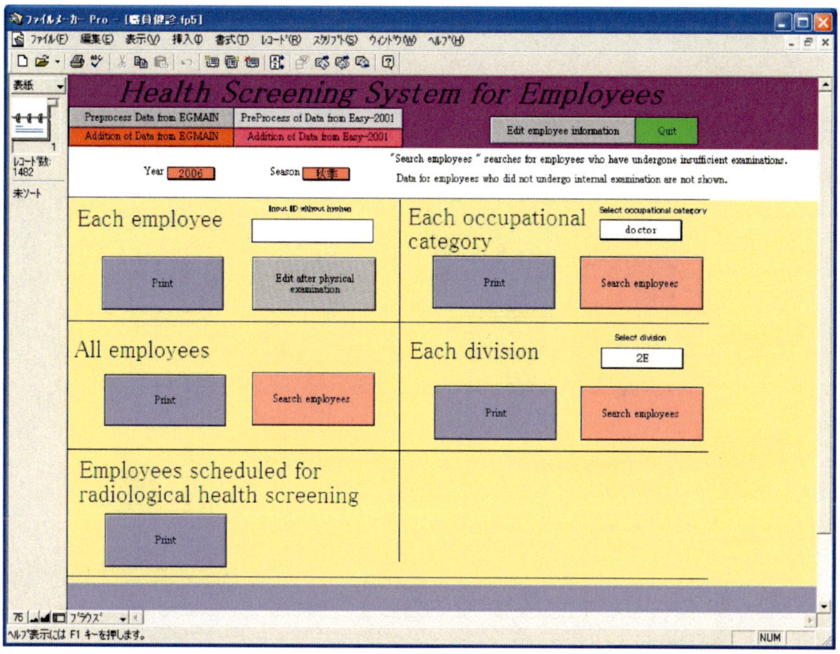

Figure 1: Start menu of this new system included in the file for examination data (D). The figure has been modified slightly because words included in the figure have been translated into English.

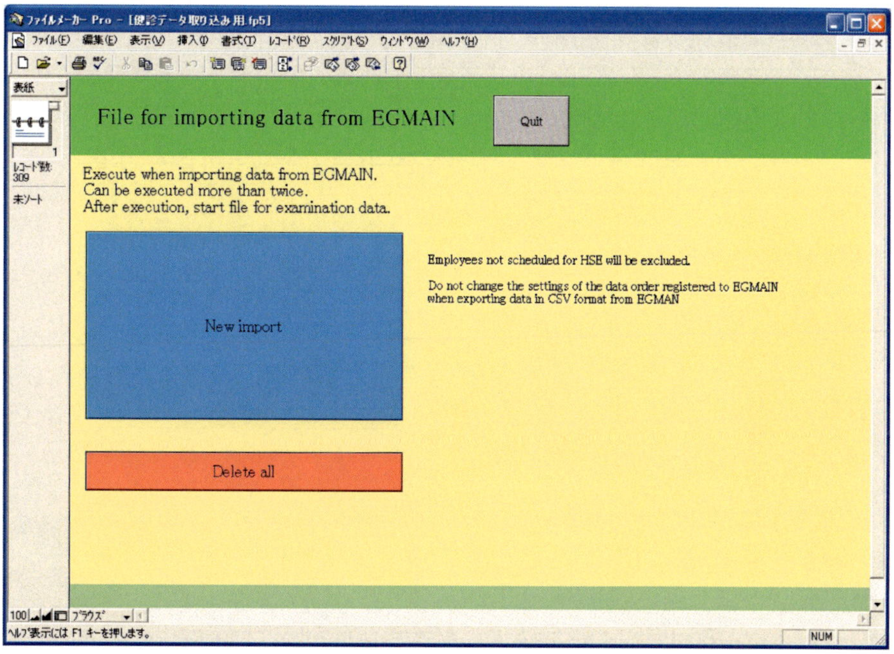

Figure 2: Start menu of the file for importing data from the order entry system (B). The figure has been modified slightly because words included in the figure have been translated into English.

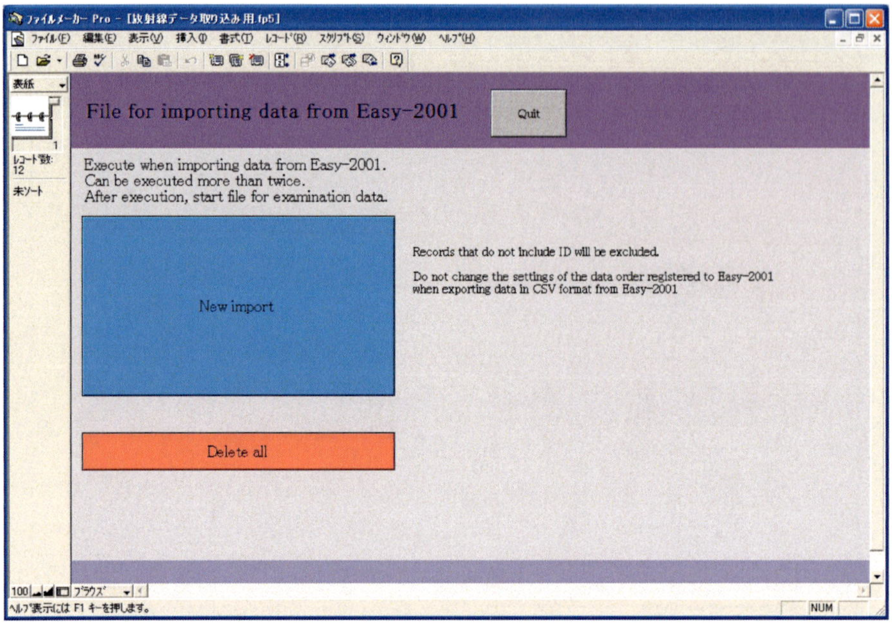

Figure 3: Start menu of the file for importing data from the radiological health screening system (C). The figure has been modified slightly because words included in the figure have been translated into English.

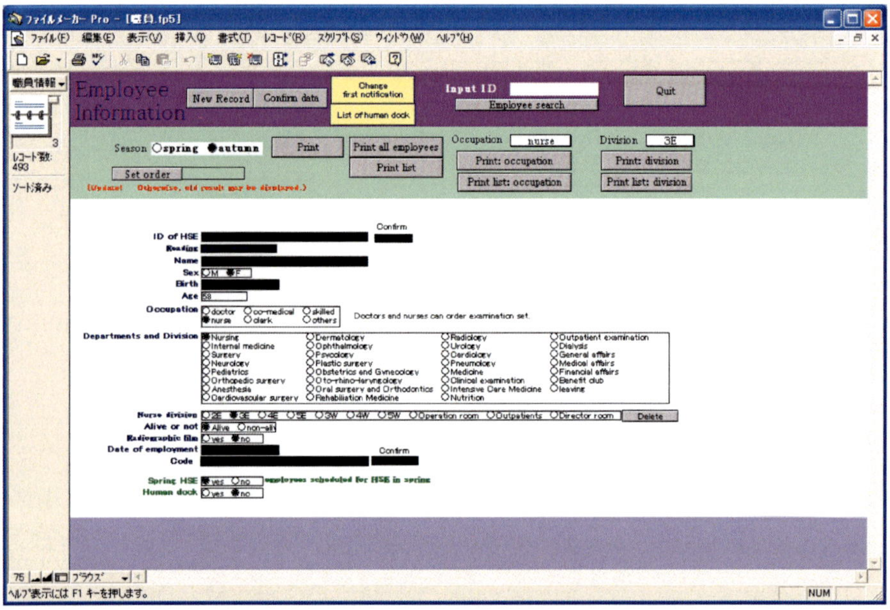

Figure 4: Start menu of the file for employee information (A). The figure has been modified slightly because words included in the figure have been translated into English. Private information is redacted. The final notification paper is the same printout.

2.2. Health Screening Workflow before Introducing this System

1) The staff in charge of the Division of General Affairs decide the screening schedule for each employee manually and distribute the first paper-based notification.

2) The staff in charge of the Division of Clinical Laboratories register employees with the clinical laboratory system directly based on the decision of the staff in charge of the Division of General Affairs.

3) The staff in charge of the Division of General Affairs distribute specimen containers from the clinical laboratory system to each employee.

4) Employees undergo physical examinations prior to internal medical examinations, and the results are transcribed manually from the clinical laboratory system onto a paper-based screening report by the staff in charge of the Division of General Affairs.

5) Prior to internal medical examinations in cases in which they are necessary, data from the radiological health screening system are transcribed manually onto a paper-based screening report by the staff in charge of the Division of General Affairs.

6) Prior to internal medical examinations in cases in which they are necessary, employees undergo an ophthalmologic and/or otologic examination, and their results are transcribed manually onto a paper-based screening report by the staff in charge of each department.

7) When undergoing internal medical examinations, each employee records his or her body weight, height, and blood pressure on a paper-based screening report.

8) The examinations are performed by an internal medical specialist who records the results on paper-based screening reports.

9) The staff in charge of the Division of General Affairs transcribe examination reports written by internal medical specialists onto final paper-based notifications, which are then distributed to the employees.

2.3. Health Screening Workflow after Introducing this System

The health screening workflow was modified as described below. Points number 4), 5), and 6) were not changed.

1) The staff in charge of the Division of General Affairs distribute a paper-based first notification to each employee on which is automatically printed a set of screening schedules for that employee using the file for employee information (A).

2) Each employee orders their own screening schedule using the order entry system.

   An ID number is specially prepared for HSE.

3) After physical examinations, the staff in charge of the Division of General Affairs receive a diskette with the results in CSV format from the staff in charge of the Division of Clinical Laboratories. CSV format data from the radiological screening system are exported to diskette by the staff in charge of the Division of General Affairs. Various examination results are printed automatically on a paper-based screening report (Fig. **5**) with the file for examination data (D) by the staff in charge of the Division of General Affairs, after CSV format data are imported with the file for importing data from (B) the order entry system (B) and/or the radiological health screening system (C).

4) Prior to internal medical examinations in cases in which they are necessary, employees undergo an ophthalmologic and/or otolaryngological examination, and their results are transcribed manually onto a paper-based screening report by the staff in charge of each department.

5) When undergoing internal medical examinations, each employee records their body weight, height, and blood pressure on a paper-based screening report.

6) The examinations are performed by an internal medical specialist who records the results on paper-based screening reports.

7) The staff in charge of the Division of General Affairs feeds internal medical examination reports into the file for examination data (D) before the final paper-based notification for each employee is printed automatically and distributed to the appropriate employee.

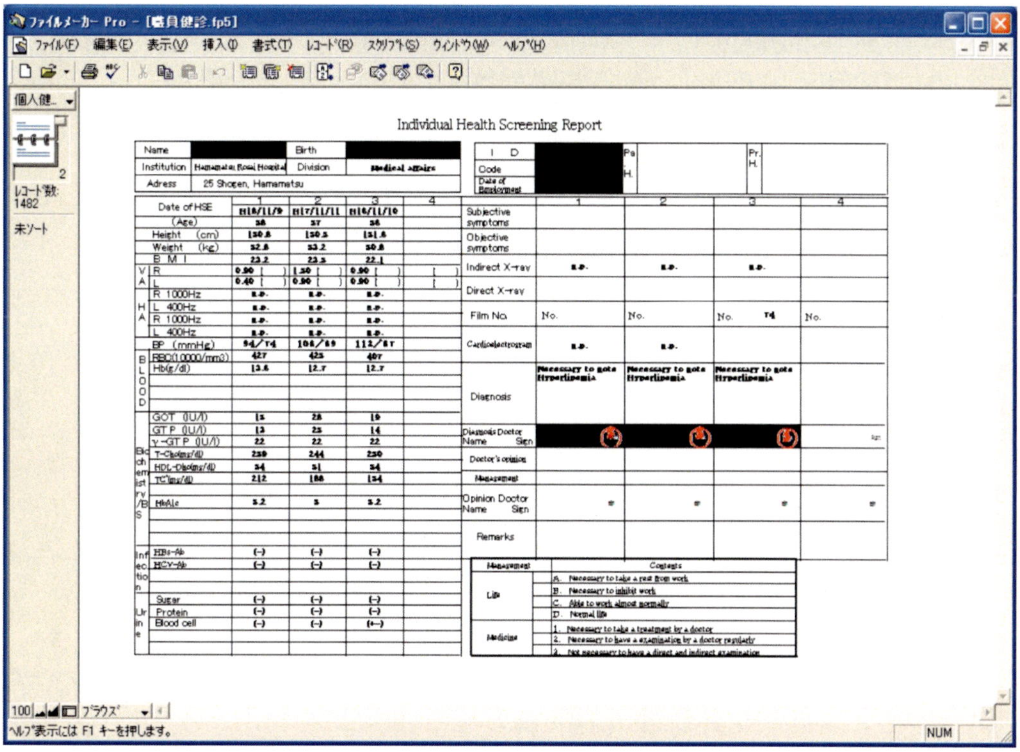

Figure 5: Screening paper printed from the file for examination data (D). The figure has been modified slightly because words included in the figure have been translated into English. Private information is redacted. The final notification paper is the same printout.

2.4. Implementation of HSE

As employees usually do not change their occupational category but sometimes change the division to which they belong, which is especially true for nurses, the file for employee information was updated whenever necessary. HSE was implemented in spring and autumn from June 1st to June 30th and from November 1st to November 30th every year, respectively.

Based on the HR regulations, the following employees were scheduled for HSE in spring: those alternating among three groups in each division (*e.g.*, nurses belonging to one of three groups in a division), those returning from maternity leave, those who changed their division from inpatient to outpatient care, those who worked more than 80 h overtime in the last 6 months, and those who worked on overnight duty more than four times in the last 6 months. All employees were scheduled for HSE in autumn. Those who had undergone in-hospital examinations after the last HSE, called "ningen dokku" ("human dock") in Japan, were not scheduled for HSE and underwent only radiological health screening.

The physical examination schedule was different for each employee. Examinations of those aged both 35 and 40 or above must include blood cells, general biochemistry, blood sugar, and urine tests. Examinations for those in other age groups exclude blood cell and general biochemistry analyses. Chest X-ray, visual and hearing acuity testing, and electrocardiogram were implemented only in autumn. The latter two tests were performed in employees aged both 35 and 40 or above. Radiological health screening was done in both spring and autumn.

2.5. Functions of a New Health Screening System for Employees

2.5.1. File for Employee Information (A)

To determine the examination schedule for each employee automatically, the following data were fed into the file for employee information: the employee's name, date of birth, occupational category, division, work status (active, retired, or suspended), use of radiographic film, HSE in spring, and whether the employee had undergone a "human dock" health checkup since the last HSE (A).

2.5.2. File for Importing Data from the Order Entry System (B) and File for Importing Data from the Radiological Health Screening System (C)

Data import from the order entry system was not always done only once, as blood and urine examinations were not always performed at the same time because employees were too busy to undergo these examinations at the same time, and because some employees underwent re-examinations or examinations outside the specified period for HSE. On the other hand, data import from the radiological health screening system (C) was usually done only once during HSE because the processing of radiographic film exposure was consigned to a third party vendor. However, it was unknown which data would be imported first into the file for examination data (D). Therefore, regardless of which data were imported first, and even if data import was repeated, scripts were developed with FileMaker Pro for pre-processing so that no contradiction would occur. That is, a new FileMaker Pro card for an employee was added only once and the examination data were updated on this card.

2.5.3. File for Examination Data (D)

The results of internal medical examinations, such as abnormalities on chest X-rays, hypertension, anemia, *etc.*, are fed into the file for examination data (D). Additional results can be fed *via* the keyboard. Examination data are common for both the general health and radiological screening schedules. All examination data are displayed in the HSE time series, and are printed separately for each employee, occupational category, division, employees scheduled for radiological health screening, or all employees. The system also includes a function to retrieve employees who have undergone insufficient examinations.

3. RESULTS

The results of HSE are shown in Fig. **5**. The total number of employees at HR from June 2004 to December 2006 was 1,482. Since its introduction in spring 2004, all HSE at this hospital have been implemented with this system. Although minor changes have been made to the system at the request of the hospital staff, no serious problems have occurred during this three-year period.

Prior to the introduction of this system, HSE had been implemented with only two dedicated staff members from the Division of General Affairs and the Division of Clinical Laboratories. For only two staff members to take charge of seasonal health screening for about 500 employees represents an unreasonable workload. The introduction of the system described here has meant that this workload has disappeared, as this system means that staff in the Division of General Affairs need no longer determine the screening schedule for each employee, distribute specimen containers from the clinical laboratory system to each employee, transcribe the results of physical examinations manually from the clinical laboratory system to the paper-based screening report, or copy screening reports for each employee containing the results of internal medical examinations. Thus, the staff of the Division of General Affairs needs to do little except to distribute the first notification, input results of internal medical examinations, and distribute final notifications. Moreover, staff in the Division of Clinical Examination became unnecessary. An additional advantage of this system is that it produces a final notification for each employee that includes the results of HSE printed in time series. This system may be useful for the staff in charge of HSE at other hospitals that do not yet have any systematization.

The system described here cost about 800,000 yen to develop, with this budget going to a vendor to process data from the order entry system to diskette in CSV format.

4. DISCUSSION

4.1. Development of the Present System

Another in-house health screening system for employees using existing systems—a management system for the Division of General Affairs and a clinical laboratory system—has been reported previously in Japan [10]. In the present report, we described our new in-house health screening system for employees that makes use of existing order entry and radiological health screening systems. The necessity of exporting data from two systems on each update of examination data may be slightly troublesome, but it was more important in this case to lower the cost of development; it would not have been possible to introduce this system if the cost had exceeded one million yen. The low development costs of the present system facilitated the systematization of HSE and secured the consent of the managers at HR to introduce the system.

The system described here is paper-based, but can also be utilized as an electronic-based system if all the necessary data, such as height, weight, blood pressure, and/or results of internal medical examinations, are fed directly. However, at HR, an electronic-based system would not be as useful because it would increase the workload for the doctors of internal medicine.

The system developed here uses general database software, and can be re-used with only slight customization of files developed with FileMaker Pro at hospitals where necessary data can be exported from existing systems. The present system is simple but useful, and has sufficient functions for HSE implementation.

Prior to the development of this system, HR received an estimated 8 million yen from a vendor for the cost of developing a customized order entry system to allow the implementation of HSE with an order entry system. This was far in excess of what HR could afford to introduce such a system. However, the cost of the present system was only about 10% of the vendor's estimate, and this was paid only to process data from the order entry system to diskette.

4.2. Problems with this System

There are a number of common problems with systems or software developed by medical staff or in-house, many of which are related to security and management [11, 12]. The present system should not be susceptible to problems of access from the outside, such as virus infections, as it is embedded within a closed network. The files used in this system have been managed by staff of the Division of General Affairs and they have been opened only during HSE, so there will be no problems caused by employees, such as the data loss. Therefore, we feel that this system has no problems related to security.

However, there may be some problems related to management as the developer of this system is the staff who left HR in July 2005 to work at another hospital. However, three years have passed since then and there have been no problems with the system at HR. Two other employees were trained as administrators of this system, and they could use FileMaker Pro before the staff left HR. In fact, these employees have made minor changes over the last three years.

FileMaker Pro has the advantage that it can be used easily by anyone, which is one of the reasons why a number of systems or software developed by medical staff with FileMaker Pro have been reported recently in Japan [13-20].

5. CONCLUSIONS

The system described here can be introduced at other hospitals at a low cost, provided an existing order entry system is in use for HSE and the hospital has one license for FileMaker Pro and FileMaker Server each.

This system is very useful and has sufficient functions for HSE. It may also be useful at hospitals where vendor-developed health screening systems for employees cannot be introduced due to budget constraints.

CONFLICT OF INTEREST

None declared.

ACKNOWLEDGEMENTS

This system was presented at the 25th Joint Conference on Medical Informatics 2005 in Japan and the 45th Annual Congress of Japan Society for Healthcare Administration 2007. The authors are grateful to the researchers present at these conferences for their comments. The authors are also grateful to the engineers of Fujitsu Chubu Systems for advice at Hamamatsu Rosai Hospital.

REFERENCES

[1] Sumitomo Cement Computer Systems Co., Ltd., http://www.sumitem.co.jp/pca/sol-health/intro.html (2010.8.12)
[2] Ishikawa Computing Center Co., Ltd., http://www.icc.co.jp/product/medical/kenkou/index_kinou.html (2010.8.12)
[3] Noteware Co., Ltd., http://www.noteware.com/ (2010.8.12)
[4] NAIS Co., Ltd., http://www.naiscorp.co.jp/ (2010.8.12)
[5] SUN PLANNING SYSTEMS Co., Ltd., http://www.sunplanning.co.jp/product/healthcare /index.html (2010.8.12)
[6] NEC Nexsolutions, Ltd., http://www.nec-nexs.com/sl/sol/admety.html (2010.8.12)
[7] Chuo Joho Systems Co., Ltd., http://www.cisys.co.jp/index_1_1_1.html (2010.8.12)
[8] TechnoLabo Co.,Ltd., http://www.tlabo.com/products/tlabo_mc.html (2010.8.12)
[9] TAK Co., Ltd., http://www.taknet.co.jp/kenshin/index.html (2010.8.12)
[10] Okamoto Y, Kawabata K, Hirai M, *et al.* Effects of collaboration the management system for general affairs and the clinical examination system –Development of health screening system for employees–. Japan Journal of Medical Informatics 1999; 19(Suppl.):608-609.
[11] Wakamiya S, Imada K, Matsunami K, *et al.* Current state and prospect of software for medical use developed by medical staff. Journal of Japanese Society for Clinical Pathway 2006; 8(2):183-189.
[12] Wakamiya S. Possibility and prospect of software for medical use developed by medical staff, Journal of Japanese Society for Clinical Pathway 2006; 8(2):171-175.

[13] Yoshida S. Patient condition adaptive path system using FileMaker Pro. Journal of Japan Society for Health Care Management 2005; 6:555-560.

[14] Yoshida S, Nakagawa N, Mimasu S. Patient database "Files for management of hospitalization" using FileMaker Pro. Journal of the Japan Pediatrics Society 1999; 103:287.

[15] Yoshida S. Database for enuresis using FileMaker Pro. Enuresis 2001; 6:27-31.

[16] Yoshida S, Hashimoto H, Narabayashi N. Management files for neonatal infant using FileMaker Pro. Journal of Japan Society for Health Care Management 2005; 530-535.

[17] Gamo M, Niida T, Hirata S, *et al.* Implementation of network database system using FileMaker Pro as subsystem of electronic medical records. Journal of Japanese Society for Clinical Pathway 2005; 7(3):485.

[18] Nakamura T, Hitsuichi H. Cooperation between the hospital information system and the system developed with FileMaker Pro. Journal of Japanese Society for Clinical Pathway 2005; 7(3):486.

[19] Hotokezaka S, Noguchi Y. Case of access log management within hospital information system using FileMaker Pro. Journal of Japanese Society for Clinical Pathway 2005; 7(3):486.

[20] Matsunami K. Supporting system of medical treatment using FileMaker Pro–Clinical pathways and DPC–. Journal of Japanese Society for Clinical Pathway 2005; 7(3):487.

CHAPTER 11

Merits and Demerits in End User Computing Based Online Incident Reporting Application Made With FileMaker Pro in Comparison With Organized Computing Based Counterpart

Shunsuke Hotokezaka*

Saga Prefectural Hospital Koseikan, 1-12-9 Mizugae, Saga, Saga, Japan

Abstract: Safety management in the medical world has become critical and many trials are reported. Our hospital renewed our safety management system in May 2005, and worked on the safety management using the online incident reporting application (OIRA) that we developed with FileMaker Pro. OIRA made the trouble information available to the hospital staff, and at the same time, we worked on access management to the database that varies record by record. Installation of OIRA was successful and in use without serious system trouble. However, in 2007, we experienced the incident reporting application replacement due to the hospital information system (HIS) replacement. After the installation of the vendor application, several inconveniences were noted. There are always controversies over end user computing (EUC) application use in the medical scene, while organized computing (OC) application is also provided by vendors that might meet the business needs. After experiencing both environments, we concluded that both EUC and OC have merits and demerits. It seems that if the speed of development, usability and flexibility of EUC are provided with a stable developing and supporting environment of OC, the computing will provide an even greater benefit.

Keywords: FileMaker Pro, incident report, end user computing, organized computing, merit, demerit, safety management, online incident reporting application, access management, record access management, on-screen help, usability, adaptability, maintenance.

1. INTRODUCTION

Safety management in the medical world has become critical and many trials are reported. Our hospital renewed our safety management system in May 2005, and worked on the safety management using the online incident reporting application (OIRA) that we developed with FileMaker Pro. OIRA made the trouble

***Address correspondence to Shunsuke Hotokezaka:** Department of Orthopedics, Saga Prefectural Hospital Koseikan, Japan; E-mail: hotokezs@ortho.med.kyushu-u.ac.jp

Shunji Wakamiya, Kazunobu Yamauchi and Hiroyuki Yoshihara (Eds)

information available to the hospital staff, and at the same time, we worked on access management to the database that varies record by record. Installation of OIRA was successful because we conducted a training seminar for safety managers on how to use OIRA prior to its inception. We handed out printed manuals as well as projected the user interfaces that the staff would use after following the manuals.

After using the system for one year, no serious system troubles were reported by the staff. OIRA training for the staff hired in the middle of the work year was left to the safety managers in the section. In order to simplify the education process, printed manuals were provided that showed the basic rules, including instructions on how to use the on-screen manuals when lost.

The safety management system with OIRA was reported in the 25th through 29th Joint Conference on Medical Informatics [1-6]. OIRA was improved not only to give the trouble or incident information to the hospital staff promptly, but also to give the real-time sum table display, which reduced the workload of safety managers.

In 2007, we experienced the incident reporting application replacement due to the hospital information system (HIS) replacement. The HIS replacement specification included the incident reporting system. The incident reporting application that we developed was virtually flawless and complaint-free; however, we had to separately maintain the software and hardware related to the incident reporting system which was more costly. There was no choice for the replacement. In fact, after the installation of the vendor application, several inconveniences were noted. There are always controversies over end user computing (EUC) application use in the medical scene; while organized computing (OC) applications are also provided by vendors that might meet the business needs. We experienced both environments and are ready to describe both the merits and demerits of EUC and OC applications.

The application that we developed with FileMaker Pro will be presented in the view points of the method of access management to incident reports' usability with on-screen help function. The merits and demerits of both the EUC and OC environments will also be discussed.

2. THE METHOD OF ACCESS MANAGEMENT TO INCIDENT REPORTS USING FILEMAKER Pro

(General Specification of the Incident Reporting System)

The basic concept of designing OIRA consisted of accessibility, ease of use, speed of reporting, access to incident information, and most importantly, privacy.

OIRA was developed with FileMaker Pro because we had already developed many tools with the software and had enough knowledge to develop the application in a relatively short period. OIRA was carefully designed to protect the privacy of not only patients but also the staff who related to each incident.

Our intranet is NOT connected to the internet for information privacy and safety reasons, thus we did not have to consider illegal external access to our intranet.

Staff are allowed to make reports regardless of their level of accessibility. Once the username and password are put into the intended fields, the registered staff name is identified from the ID management file (Figs. **1, 2**).

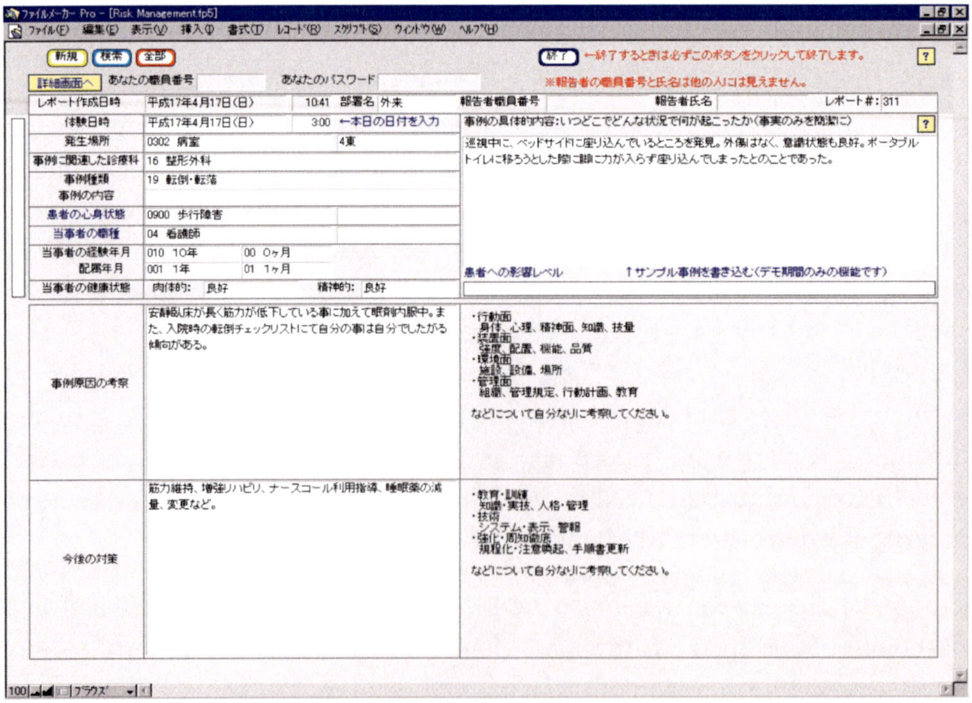

Figure 1: Username and Password Input (whole screen).

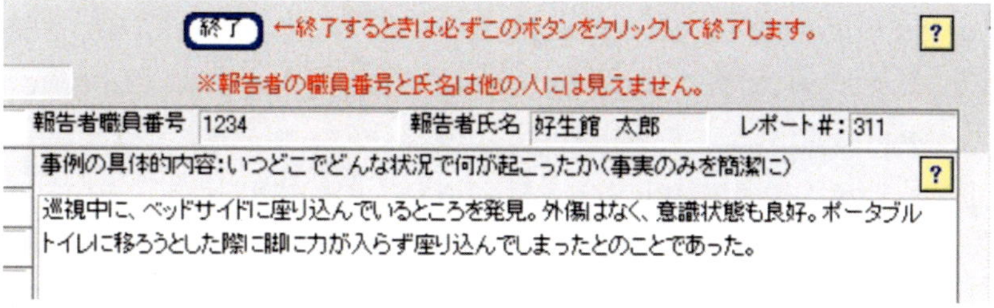

Figure 2: Username and Password Input (close look of the screen).

Once the record (report) is closed, both the username and password fields are locked, and the next time the report is accessed, the user will see a similar layout, but without the username and password fields (Fig. **3**). The first reporter has priority of access management.

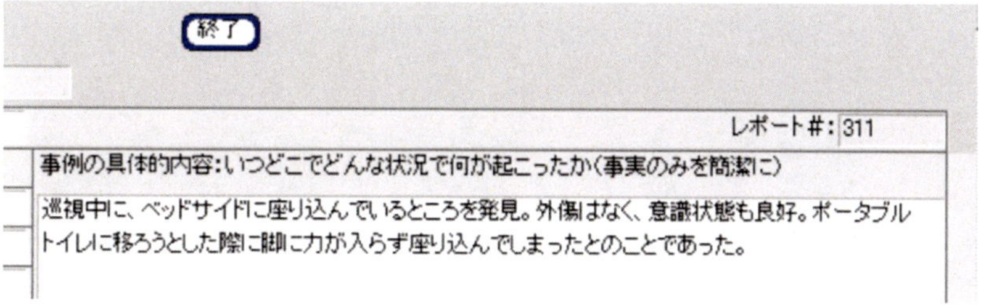

Figure 3: Layout without Username and Password fields.

The default setting of the new report is set to "closed", which means the report is not completed, and only the reporter and the safety managers have access to the report. If the report is accessed by someone other than the reporter, the layout does not display the reporter's name, as shown in Fig. **3**, thus no one will know who wrote the report.

After the initial report is made, the safety manager will review the content and appropriateness of the report. If any privacy information is included, the safety manager will delete it and complete the report, then change the status of the report to "open".

Regular reports are usually reported by only one staff member; however, in some instances more than one staff member is needed to complete a report. For example, more than one witness of an incident may exist, or someone might have to make the initial report in place of the witness for occupational reasons, or more than one person might be involved in the incident and more than one person might have to help to complete the incident report. The OIRA had to be designed not only for the accessibility of reporters and safety managers, but also for the accessibility of some other related staff report by report. For this purpose, an additional layout was provided which allows a reporter to grant certain staff members access to the report. The additional layout also displays the access log showing who accessed the report. Subscripts that make a new record in the log file are also provided as a FileMaker Pro file, with information of the user who is currently accessing the report. Day, time and action are programmed to run ahead of each script of the intended action (Fig. **4**).

本事例のアクセス状況

アクセスログは重要な操作について全て保存されます。

アクセス設定

2005/6/4	7:41:31	EIK03	●●職員番号:1234 詳細画面へ展開し閲覧
2005/6/4	7:41:25	EIK03	「レベル2」に設定してあった影響度分類を「レベル
2005/6/4	7:41:19	EIK03	●●職員番号:1234 詳細画面へ展開し閲覧
2005/6/4	7:41:11	EIK03	●職員番号:1234 非公開の標準画面へ展開し閲
2005/6/4	7:39:15	佛坂 俊輔	●●職員番号:10708 詳細画面へ展開し閲覧
2005/6/4	7:38:46	佛坂 俊輔	「レベル1」に設定してあった影響度分類を「レベル
2005/6/4	7:37:55	佛坂 俊輔	●●職員番号:123415 詳細画面へ展開し閲覧
2005/6/4	7:37:13	佛坂 俊輔	●職員番号:123415 非公開の標準画面へ展開し
2005/6/4	7:36:35	佛坂 俊輔	標準画面から一覧へ
2005/6/4	7:21:38	佛坂 俊輔	●●職員番号:10708 詳細画面へ展開し閲覧
2005/6/4	7:21:25	佛坂 俊輔	●職員番号:1234 非公開の標準画面へ展開し閲
2005/6/4	7:13:37	EIK03	●職員番号:1234 非公開の標準画面へ展開し閲
2005/6/4	7:12:42	EIK03	●●職員番号:10708 詳細画面へ展開し閲覧
2005/6/4	7:12:06	EIK03	●職員番号:10708 非公開の標準画面へ展開し
2005/6/4	7:11:11	EIK03	●●職員番号:10708 詳細画面へ展開し閲覧

Figure 4: Log file of report accesses.

Ten fields are provided for additional report access (Fig. **5**). When extra staff's access has to be set for the report, the initial reporter will feed certain related staff's number (5 digits) in one of the fields, allowing the staff to access the report. This function is also provided by a script that runs when a user clicks on a layout-switching button from a list of reports to each report. The script will lead the user to the username and password input layout. After the username and password match is confirmed by the related ID management file, the script also checks if 1) the user is the initial reporter 2) the user is one of the safety managers or 3) the user was granted access by the initial reporter. If one of these conditions is cleared, the user will be allowed to see the report, otherwise the access will be denied. This scripting for access management made it possible to allow as many as 10 related staff members to access the report if necessary, while no other reports will be accessed if it is not necessary.

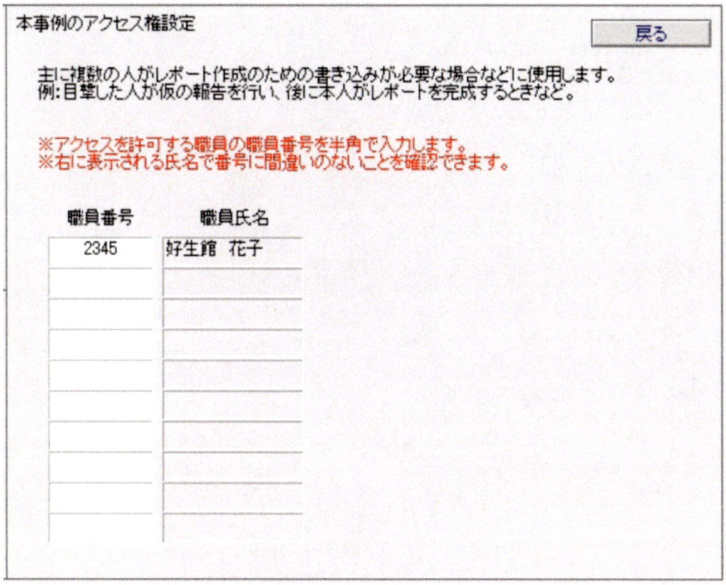

Figure 5: Ten fields are provided for up to 10 staffs' access.

3. ON-SCREEN HELP FUNCTION

Another featured function of the OIRA is the on-screen help buttons. At the initial installation of OIRA, we conducted a training seminar for safety managers on how to use OIRA. We handed out printed manuals as well as projected the user interfaces that staffs would use after following the manuals.

However, some staff is hired in the middle of the work year, and their education of how to use OIRA is left to the safety managers in the section. In order to simplify the education process, we prepared printed manuals that show basic rules including how to use on-screen manual when lost.

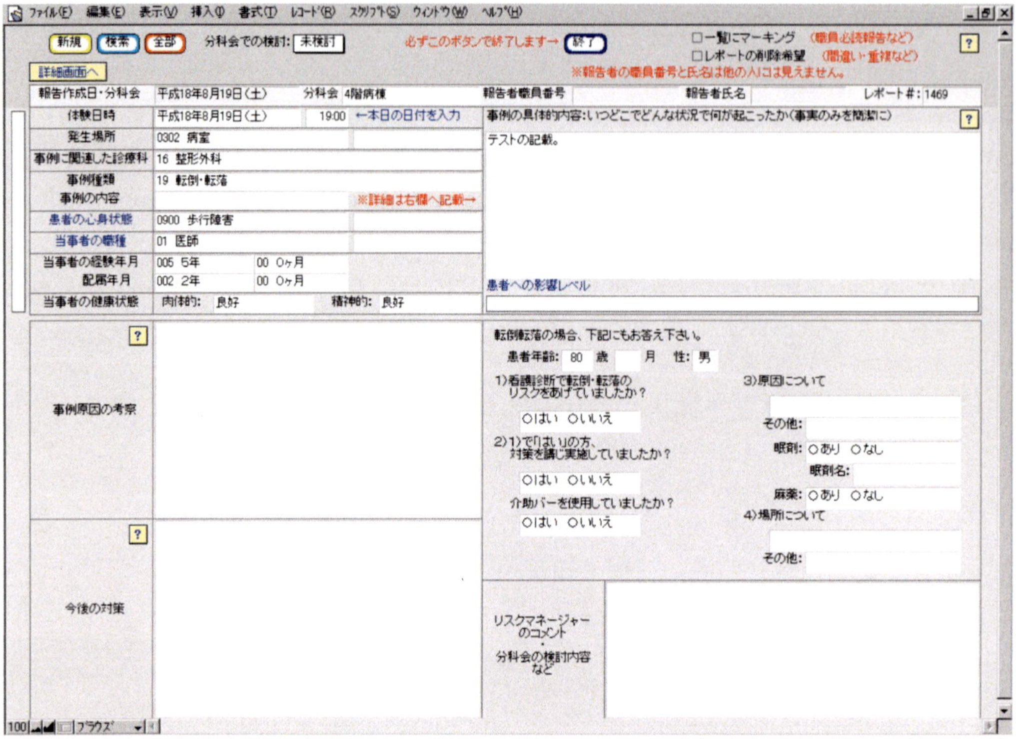

Figure 6A: The standard reporting screen.

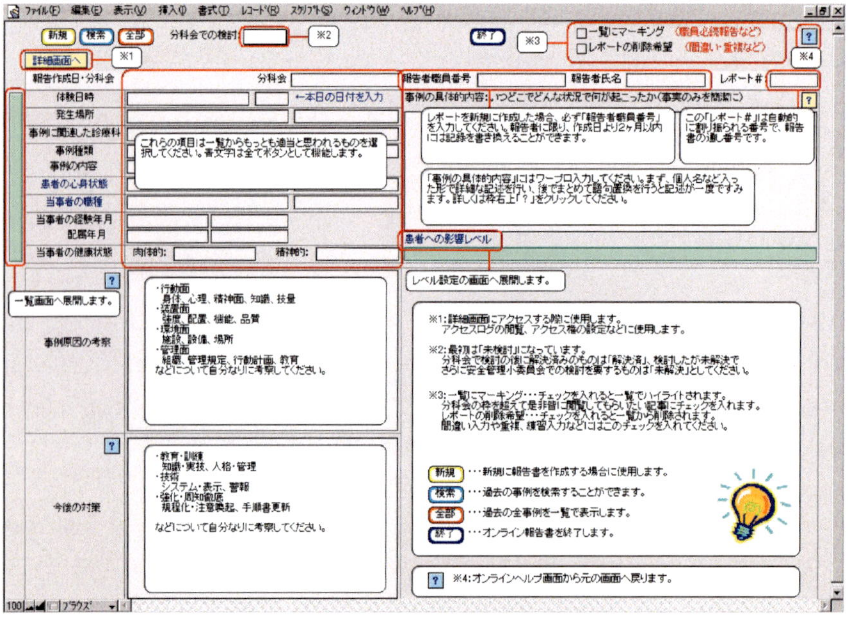

Figure 6B: The standard reporting screen with "?" button clicked.

On all the screens that a user will use, there is an on-screen "?" button either in the upper right corner or near certain fields where users are likely to get lost. This helps lost users to easily find out where to go. (Fig. **6A**, **6B**). The help screen is like balloon help, but balloon help was not chosen as the tool to make the help screens. Balloon help is a useful function, but it appears only when the target is crossed over: a lost user has to cross over each object until the correct button is found. Our help function differs from balloon help in that all the manual scripts are written statically on the screen. Lost users can scan the entire screen very quickly in order to find out where to go to accomplish their task. It seems the help button worked very well because there was virtually no question about how to use OIRA.

4. MERITS AND DEMERITS OF EUC APPLICATION AND OC APPLICATION

The OIRA was operating successfully, but in 2007, we had to switch to another incident reporting application due to hospital information system (HIS) replacement; the HIS replacement specification included an incident reporting system. The OC application was supposed to be the same in terms of functionality and usability, but it seems that both our OIRA made from EUC and the incident reporting application provided from OC (IRAOC) have merits and demerits which must be considered when installing such systems of safety management.

After the replacement of the application, the first difficulty encountered was in the data input. The input interface was provided by a web browser with IRAOC, and the pages were too long to be completed within a single screen, so “scrolling” down was necessary, which is not as easy or efficient as the “tab” switching that we adopted for OIRA.

Check boxes are given to select the category in which the case belongs and whether or not the case is related. OIRA had a relatively simple interface in which to choose such categories.

In cases of falling, IRAOC seemed to have a couple of similar check boxes. Monthly statistical reports made from IRAOC revealed that one specific check box MUST be checked in order to be counted as a falling case, while other check boxes were not counted. This inconvenience is partly because of the guidance from the Ministry of Health, Labor and Welfare and partly because of the design of the application.

Another inconvenience we encountered was in cases which did not belong to a particular patient and could not be reported in IRAOC form because it did not allow us to omit patient ID information, regardless of the case. This issue was resolved after negotiations with the IRAOC vendor. On-screen help functions or manuals were not available with the IRAOC. Reporters had to refer to the printed manuals when they needed assistance.

After all these inconveniences, we listed the merits and demerits of both OIRA (EUC application) and IRAOC (OC application). They are listed below from several different viewpoints.

4.1. Adaptability

Changes can be made quickly with the EUC application, especially when using a flexible database software like FileMaker Pro which we adopted to develop OIRA. Most of the changes can be performed almost immediately. However, changes to the application improvement and customization of OC application will require a discussion and negotiation process which cost a tremendous amount of time and money.

4.2. Security and Maintenance

While EUC applications are adaptable, it could mean the changes might be performed without sufficient discussion. The EUC application developer's personal viewpoints or philosophy might factor into the design of the software, which might be hard to maintain if a change in the application's designer or programmer is made. OC applications, on the other hand, are usually well discussed and inspected by a group of people before making a change, and will be more stable in maintenance since such applications are much less personally affected.

4.3. Design

In many cases, EUC applications are created from the local end-users' needs by someone who is good at programming and in touch with the users' needs, or by users acting as their own programmers. Usability comes to the forefront in this kind of situation because the programmer is very familiar with the workflow and the application of the program can be designed to be used very easily.

However, consideration must be given to the possibility that the EUC programming environment could lead to a slanted application design based on the programmer's software philosophy.

In the OC environment, usability is very difficult to be expressed in terms of specifications and even if the specifications are perfectly matched, many difficulties might be encountered after the installation of the application.

However, OC applications will be thoroughly discussed and designed by a team of end-users, workflow managers, system engineers and programmers, making the application more objective from many aspects.

5. CONCLUSION

As stated above, both the EUC and OC applications seem to have merits and demerits. It seems that if the speed of development, usability and flexibility of EUC are provided with a stable developing and supporting environment of OC, the computing will provide an even greater benefit.

CONFLICT OF INTEREST

None declared.

ACKNOWLEDGEMENT

None declared.

REFERENCES

[1] Hotokezaka H, Noguchi Y. Online Incident Reporting System Made with a Database Software on the Market: A Solution for Improving Access Management and Saving Preparation for Risk Management Meetings. 25th Japan Association of Medical Informatics meeting, (CD-ROM) 2005.

[2] Hotokezaka H, Noguchi Y. Online Incident Reporting System Made by a Database Software on the Market (1): Workflow Change after the System Installation and Real-Time

Sum Table Display. 26th Japan Association of Medical Informatics meeting, (CD-ROM) 2006.

[3] Hotokezaka H, Noguchi Y. On-line Incident Reporting System Made by a Database Software on the Market (2): Simplification of User Education by On-screen Assistance Interface. 26th Japan Association of Medical Informatics meeting, (CD-ROM) 2006.

[4] Hotokezaka H, Noguchi Y. On-line Consent Form Booklet Management System Made by a Database Software on the Market: Consent Form Database and Custom Booklet Creating Environment. 27th Japan Association of Medical Informatics meeting, (CD-ROM) 2007.

[5] Hotokezaka H, Noguchi Y. On-line Consent Form Booklet Preparation Assisting Tool Made by a Database Software on the Market: New Functions and Customizing Environment Improvements. 28th Japan Association of Medical Informatics meeting, (CD-ROM) 2008.

[6] Hotokezaka H, Noguchi Y. On-line Assisting Tool for Preparing Consent Form Booklets Made by a Commercially Available Database Software: Evaluation of Time Required for Making and Printing Booklet. 29th Japan Association of Medical Informatics meeting, (CD-ROM) 2009.

CHAPTER 12

The World of Software Developed by Medical Staff

Shunji Wakamiya[1,*], Kazunobu Yamauchi[2], Hiroyuki Yoshihara[3], Tsukasa Tsunoda[4] and Osamu Sato[5]

[1]Kawasaki Medical School, 577 Matsushima, Kurashiki, Okamaya, Japan; [2]Fujita Health University, 1-98 Dengakugakubo,Kutsukake,Toyoake,Aichi, Japan; [3]Graduate School of Medicine Kyoto University, Yoshida-Konoe, Sakyo-ku, Kyoto, Japan; [4]Kawasaki Medical School Hospital, 577 Matsushima, Kurashiki, Okamaya, Japan and [5]Tokyo Keizai University, 1-7-34 Minami-Machi, Kokubunji, Tokyo, Japan

Abstract: End user computing in the field of medical treatment and care has a number of peculiarities, "the world of software developed by medical staff", which is unique from the viewpoint of the range of end users and the method of management when end user computing is implemented.

Keywords: End user computing, end user applications, filemaker Pro, hospital, medical staff, world, medical treatment, care, enterprise, microsoft access, management.

End user computing in the field of medical treatment and care has a number of peculiarities, "the world of software developed by medical staff", which is unique from the viewpoint of the range of end users and the method of management when end user computing is implemented [1]. Although end user applications are often implemented throughout a whole facility in the field of medical treatment and care [2], such applications or systems are not generally found in enterprise environments [3]. Although end user applications are managed by the end users themselves in the field of medical treatment and care, they are managed by both end users and the division of information and systems in an enterprise environment [2, 3]. We presented "the world of software developed by medical staff" at the workshop "Current State and Prospects of Original Medical Systems Developed in Various Hospitals" at the IEEE/ICME International Conference on

***Address correspondence to Shunji Wakamiya:** Department of Ophthalmology, Kawasaki Medical School, Japan; E-mail: oph@mtj.biglobe.ne.jp

Complex Medical Engineering-CME2007 in Beijing, held on 23 May, 2007 [4] and the audience expressed astonishment at the idea that the disadvantages of organizational computing could be abrogated by the advantages of end user computing. We hope that this book will evoke the same response. FileMaker Pro is not the only tool utilized in end user computing in the field of medical treatment and care, but is simply one system that is preferred by many medical staff in Japan. Indeed, other hospital-introduced medical information systems have been developed using Microsoft Access. This book does not discuss the merits/demerits of developed software, the systems themselves, or the management of end user computing because the methods software and system of development and management by end user computing introduced here have not yet been established historically, and only a hypothesis is presented to efficiently improve the environment of medical treatment and care. Indeed, the method of developing software and systems introduced in this book may be lost in 20 years, and further studies are required. However, we will be glad if this book can contribute, even in a small way, to the improvement of medical treatment and care around the world.

CONFLICT OF INTEREST

None declared.

ACKNOWLEDGEMENT

None declared.

REFERENCES

[1] Wakamiya S. Possibility and prospect of software for medical use developed by medical staff, Journal of Japanese Society for Clinical Pathway 2006; 8(2): 171-175.

[2] Wakamiya S, Imada K, Matsunami K, *et al.* Current state and prospect of software for medical use developed by medical staff. Journal of Japanese Society for Clinical Pathway 2006; 8(2): 183-189.

[3] Brancheau C, Brown V. The Management of End-User Computing: Status and Direction. ACM Computing Surveys 1993; 25(4): 437-482.

[4] Wakamiya S, Yamauchi K, Kiryu J, *et al.* Management system of paper-based critical pathways developed in each hospital: Comparison between a medical school hospital and a general hospital. Conference Book of 2007IEEE/ICME International Conference on Complex Medical Engineering 2007; 319-323.

CHAPTER 13

End User Computing and FileMaker Pro Observed From the Viewpoint of Hospital Information System Management

Yoshimune Shiratori*

Gifu University Hospital, 1-1 Yanagido, Gifu, Gifu, Japan

Abstract: FileMaker Pro (FMP) which is often used for end user computing. It is a software characterized by not only user-friendliness and ease of customization, but it also has an additional aspect, being a database management software. Some general observations with regard to this topic are stated as follows: why software programs are used to this extent, what major purposes they serve for users, and whether there are any issues associated with using this type of user-friendly software program. Following are the 3 purposes of implementing FMP; 1) economical reasons, 2) where detailed development is expected to reflect user requirements, 3) as a prototype for contracts and creation. There has been a rapid progress in the information and communication technology (ICT) at hospitals in Japan for the last 10 years. In such an environment, software programs such as FMP, which is user-friendly and easy for users to customize on their own, plays a vital role. It is anticipated that it will establish itself as a software program with expandability, enabling smooth communication with vendors, rather than being viewed as a software program that poses a threat to vendors.

Keywords: Hospital information system (HIS), end user computing (EUC), system management, FileMaker, database management software, user-friendliness, customization, economic, user requirements, prototype, information and communication technology (ICT).

1. INTRODUCTION

FileMaker Pro (FMP) is a user-friendly software and database (DB) management software program that is simple and convenient for users. This software program is used across various departments at a hospital, earning the appreciation of various users [1-9]. In fact, some examples are also given in other sections of this document. Hence, I would like to provide general observations on topics such as: why such software programs are used to this extent, what major purposes they

***Address correspondence to Yoshimune Shiratori:** Medical Information Department, Gifu University Hospital, Japan; E-mail: tara@gifu-u.ac.jp serve for users, and whether there are any issues associated with using this type of user-friendly software program.

2. INFORMATION AND COMMUNICATION TECHNOLOGY (ICT) UTILIZATION AT HOSPITALS IN JAPAN

Examples of electronic charts were pioneered at hospitals in Japan from the mid-1990s, and since 2000, electronic charts have become officially adopted and widely used. Hospital Information System (HIS) follows a path of 3 stages in which it is first implemented to streamline the task of charging medical service fees, becomes an order entry system connecting departmental systems, and then generates electronic charts, but the process has been rapidly evolving in recent years. According to a joint study by Japanese Association of Healthcare Information Systems Industry (JAHIS) and the Journal of *New Medicine in Japan*, in 2007, the number of order entry system was 1,953 out of 8,874 hospitals, which accounted for 22.0%. Comparing this with the number of beds, it was 68% for more than 400 beds and 82% for more than 600 beds. In the same study, electronic charts were implemented at 848 hospitals in total, equivalent to 9.6%. When this was compared in terms of the number of beds, it was 32% for more than 400 beds and 47% for more than 600 beds [10, 11].

With the rapid progress of ICT, due to the progress and development of HIS, it is becoming possible to electronically collect and analyze data related to the medical care of a patient and management data (human resource management, medical materials/drug management, facility equipment management, *etc.,*) within the medical facilities at advanced hospitals. Based on this information, consideration is now being given to implementing a PDCA cycle, which is one of the medical management methods, at each level (overall, diagnosis and treatment department, individual *etc.,*) at a hospital.

Conversely speaking, hospitals fully equipped do not account for the majority, but it can be considered that this is a transition period in which ICTs become rapidly and widely spread at hospitals.

In the midst of significant changes such as the implementation of computers in hospitals, commencement of ordering, and computerization of medical records, roles and responsibilities that information administrators and their departments have at hospitals are also changing significantly. There are 3 fundamental tasks for which information administrators at the hospitals are responsible.

1) Network security management

   Developing an efficient network, and performing network maintenance and operation to prevent leakage of personal information, *etc.,* is a major component of this task. In relation to this, the management of user registration and access authorization, *etc.,* is also an important task.

2) Management of the entire hospital information system

   Performing system implementation and upgrades as well as maintenance and operation. From a total optimization perspective, adjusting between departmental systems is an important task. This is an essential task which has necessitated how to put users' requests into practice

3) Managing and providing data

   This is a basic operation in which the prerequisite of having data that is not altered and that maintains its authenticity is met. This is a significant part of the work because if a DB is not developed properly and data cannot be provided later, then a complaint may be made as to the purpose for which the data were saved.

3. OBJECTIVES OF IMPLEMENTING FMP

Considering the IT utilization within a hospital setting as described above, the fact has to be taken into account that user-friendly software such as FMP is being applied from the perspective of hospital information managers.

There are many hospitals that have developed a part of, if not the entire HIS by using software programs such as FMP, which can be easily handled by the users. What basically are the purposes of implementing this software program in such hospitals?

3.1. Economical Reasons

Many ICT configurations, mainly receipt computer and order entry systems, as described above, have been implemented at hospitals in Japan. However, many hospitals do not necessarily have a good balance sheet and hence, it is very difficult for many hospitals to make a substantial investment in ICT. As the unit price of HIS is substantially expensive compared to a general program, realistically speaking, there are hospitals that cannot implement all the desired configurations. For hospitals with such problems, users perform programming, customization, and repair and maintenance to obtain the configuration desired by a hospital or a user at a reasonable price.

In cases in which a system is implemented for these reasons, priority is likely given to implementing it at a low cost, and there are instances in which attention to security is insufficient, or a configuration is such that less attention is paid to laws, *etc.* Hence, it is important to take these matters into consideration. In addition, in cases in which a system is implemented under such circumstances, there are many instances where a small number of people or an individual is asked to create a configuration; hence, it is important to have a configuration in place such that it can be continuously used even after the individual leaves the hospital due to an internal transfer, or for some other plausible reason.

3.2. A Case in Which Detailed Development is Expected to Reflect User Requirements

The next biggest reason to implement FMP is to improve usability, rather than for economical reasons. If a developer and a user who carries out tasks are different individuals, it is possible that not everything is covered. To compensate for this, it is essential that sufficient interviews are conducted with vendors, or a deep understanding is effectuated of tasks performed. System developers should always be aware of user requests, develop a full understanding and consideration for such requests, and conduct further studies and research. Detailed development is often observed in user interface sections only, or in the connection parts of a mission-critical system and a configuration that a user has created, but there are cases in which the users program the entire configuration, including mission-critical systems. This document presents many actual cases; however, detailed development that users require, such as these cases, can be often categorized into the following 3 patterns.

3.2.1. User-Friendly Interface Designed to be Easy to Navigate for Beginners

New members of staff join a hospital on a regular basis, and especially, doctors often change hospitals within a short period of time, and it is also not rare for doctors to work at multiple hospitals at one time. It is, hence, desirable that a configuration is in place so that even such new staff can perform tasks without spending too much time on operation training or reading manuals, use operational procedures that are easy to follow, and use them with little time spent on practicing, in a safe manner, and without making any mistakes. It is necessary to make every effort to reduce situations that confuse users about operations, such as not understanding which button to press. Needless to say, basic considerations should be taken into account, such as having a simple hierarchy and placing buttons at visible locations. It is necessary to pay attention to differences in perceptions between program developers on the vendor side, and users who do not have extensive knowledge about ICT.

3.2.2. Realization of Natural Business Flows for Users

It is apparent that medical-related procedures are often not familiar to the general public (including engineers who program), and there are cases in which exact matches are not observed with respect to business flows. This causes substantial stress to users. Instances in which procedural flows such as a medical treatment do not match screen operations, and cases in which users do not understand how doctors make decisions based on what principles and how they lead to the next action to be taken, cause screens to interfere with the natural flow of thought. It is not preferable for users to have to go back to a previous screen, or to look for a required screen for operational purposes, due to these reasons. Moreover, in terms of preventing the natural flow of thought, it is also not desirable for users to have to wait for several minutes due to the slow processing time of computers. For a configuration in which these events are required, it is expected that users will strongly request a configuration that can reflect their own thinking.

3.2.3. Automation of Routine Tasks

There are many cases in which people who perform the task make one choice primarily, although logically speaking there are many choices available. When it comes to making decisions, one choice may not necessarily be made primarily, but often, decisions are made this way, and on an exceptional basis, other cases are selected. Hence, including such cases, there is a substantial number of routine operations. In such cases, users hope that they can perform those tasks as easily as possible. Specifically, users hope to reduce the number of clicks they perform in the system as much as possible. Hence, it is natural that users raise such requests as: when this task is performed, it is generally performed after that task, and so we would like to automate that task. This type of request is not noticed during the development phase or the requirements definition phase, and it is not rare to encounter this type of request after a system is implemented and is running. Considering this, users tend to prefer a configuration which they can freely customize on their own. Whether minor issues that are discovered afterward can be reflected in the system or not can have a significant impact on usability.

There are 2 considerations that need careful attention in such situations. Firstly, regarding routine tasks, there are many exceptions in the medical world. There are cases in which non-routine tasks are allowed in cases that involve human lives. Taking such cases into consideration, it is necessary to have flexibility in dealing with exceptional cases. Secondly, it is necessary to carefully assess whether or not automation and simplification could increase risks associated with medical accidents. It is not acceptable that something that can be prevented if a person (medical care provider) acting as an intermediary surpasses any checks on the system operation side, and due to automation, this leads to medical accidents. There are many reported cases of accidents caused by human error, and one of the objectives of automation is to prevent human errors, but the opposite holds true at times. Program developers need to consider that business flow automation could lead to a reduction in the check functions performed, namely, by humans, and study the impact carefully from an operational perspective in advance.

3.3. A Role as a Prototype for Contracts and Creation

Users create programs, not always necessarily to replace the role of vendors. It seems that this can be an effective method for users to jointly collaborate with vendors and communicate information that vendors do not have, from users to vendors.

As mentioned above, in general, as a system implementation is performed, vendors and users discuss with each other, and perform any necessary adjustments as the implementation progresses. However, in reality, there is a gap in terms of awareness between vendors and users that cannot always be spanned. Due to this, in cases in which users want to have this type of item designed, or users and vendors want to sign a contract based on that type of creation, it is substantially possible that it may lead to a misunderstanding between both parties if it is based solely on verbal discussions. These gaps are often addressed by documents such as specifications and contracts and by discussions between both parties. If a prototype, which does not have to be a complete product, is available, and users and vendors are in a situation where they can understand a configuration in more detail, it will lead to the following improvement: reducing the possibility of misunderstanding, reducing the amount of time and energy spent on meetings, *etc.*, and increasing the possibility of implementing what users request.

For the creation of a prototype, it is of course preferred for it to be as close to a complete product as possible; however, it does not always necessarily have to be in a complete form, as long as it is in a form that can be used for explanation purposes and for improving understanding on both sides. If an ideal system is something that users can easily customize and not a complete system, then it is possible to leave problems that users find hard to deal with, such as security problems and robustness of the system, as they are and let the vendors handle them. It seems that this is a possible path toward improving a product by leveraging users' strengths in business processes and vendors' expertise through collaboration with vendors, and jointly supporting each other.

4. FROM THE VIEWPOINT OF DB MANAGEMENT WITHIN A HOSPITAL

FMP is a software characterized by not only user-friendliness and ease of customization, but it also has an additional aspect, namely that of being DB management software. What will happen if the utilization of FMP is considered by placing a focus on this type of perspective, based on the point of view of a hospital information administrator?

4.1. A Case in Which it is Used as a Part of a Mission-Critical System by Directly Connecting Directly to a Mission-Critical System

This means that FMP serves as a replacement for a DB management system that manages DBs such as IBM DB2, Oracle Database, Microsoft SQL Server, MySQL that are often used in mission-critical systems on computers. For this reason, with this operational method, it is essential that a configuration containing FMP reflects contents such as regulatory requirements and governmental advice. In other words, it is necessary to address requirements such as authenticity, readability, and storage capability, in addition to security as a system that is required for general HIS, system robustness, data redundancy, data continuity, data confidentiality, *etc.* FMP is faced with the requirement to satisfy criteria in the medical world, and not just serve as a general tool. It is necessary to pay attention when using FMP as a part of a mission-critical system such as this case presents, because even if the system is user-friendly, it may lose its legal standing as formal medical records.

4.2. A Case in Which DB Utilization is Promoted for Each Individual

At a clinical site, instead of situations in which a search of the entire data within a hospital by collaborating closely with a mission critical system such as Section 4.1 is expected, it is often required to create a DB related to examinations and surgeries that one performed at one's own department and then conduct a search from there. Due to this, many medical care providers and their groups prepare their own DB. Software programs such as FMP are used in such cases. In other words, it is easier and more efficient for users to manage partially specialized data extracted from a DB of the entire hospital, rather than using the entire DB each time.

As this DB generally contains information equivalent to personal information, it needs to be handled with care. Hospital information administrators could be asked to extract original data as a batch from a DB in a mission-critical system and transfer it to this DB. In this case, they need to provide advice from the perspective of personal information protection, by studying the purpose of usage and the management situation. In contrast, they may be asked to transfer data accumulated in a user's DB to a DB in a mission-critical system or electronic charts. In such cases as well, caution should be taken from the perspective of assuring authentication.

When taking this into account, there are many cases in which it is better to centrally manage a DB, rather than having users manage it separately. For this reason, there are cases in which there is a user DB such as FMP, *etc.*, kept centrally, although here they do not function as a DB of a mission-critical system directly.

5. CHALLENGES FOR THE FUTURE

There has been rapid progress in ICT at hospitals in Japan for the last 10 years. However, this has not been to an extent such that HIS can be said to have matured; hence, users continue to raise requests. In such an environment, software programs such as FMP, which is user-friendly and easy for users to customize on their own, plays a big role. End user computing becomes more important. Fundamentally, the ideal is to implement a user-based system and regardless of the system, it needs to have a configuration that is user-friendly. In that regard, FMP plays a role that HIS lacks. Unfortunately, the current situation is such that there are many areas that are not particularly desirable for hospital information administrators.

Hence, will the role of FMP be terminated as HIS matures? As presented in this document, the objectives of implementing FMP will not easily disappear. In that regard, it is expected that it will continue to be used, with a certain degree of risk. Furthermore, as described in Section 3.3, it is possible to promote sharing of both parties' understanding by becoming a "language" that connects users and vendors. Instead of terminating its role, it might contribute to further development, depending on how it is used.

It is expected that it will establish itself as a software program with expandability, which enables smooth communication with vendors, rather than being viewed as a software program that poses a threat to vendors.

CONFLICT OF INTEREST

None declared.

ACKNOWLEDGEMENT

None declared.

REFERENCES

[1] Yoshida S, Nakagawa N, Mimasu S. Patient database "Files for management of hospitalization" using FileMaker Pro. Journal of the Japan Pediatrics Society 1999; 103: 287.

[2] Yoshida S. Patient condition adaptive path system using FileMaker Pro. Journal of Japan Society for Health Care Management 2005; 6: 555-560.

[3] Gamo M, Niida T, Hirata S, *et al.* Implementation of network database system using FileMaker Pro as subsystem of electronic medical records. Journal of Japanese Society for Clinical Pathway 2005; 7: 485.

[4] Wakamiya S, Imada K, Matsunami K, *et al.* Current state and prospect of software for medical use developed by medical staff. Journal of Japanese Society for Clinical Pathway 2006; 8: 183-189.

[5] Wakamiya S. Possibility and prospect of software for medical use developed by medical staff, Journal of Japanese Society for Clinical Pathway 2006; 8: 171-175.

[6] El-Hayes K, Harrity C, Abu Zeineh T. A novel management database in obstetrics and gynaecology to introduce the electronic healthcare record and improve the clinical audit process. Stud Health Technol Inform 2006; 121: 266-75.

[7] Van Hees D, Van Gelder F. Importance of informatics and database management in transplant coordination. Acta Chir Belg 2008; 108:22-26

[8] Yamamoto Y. Construction and use of a clinical decision support system with intelligent processing as part of a real-time data warehouse. Japan Journal of Medical Informatics 2009; 29: 178-181.

[9] Yoshida S, Takahashi M, Matsunami K, *et al.* Intersystem coordination between EMR and user-made system. Japan Journal of Medical Informatics 2009; 29: 268-273.

[10] Tanaka H. EHR and IT medicine. New Medicine in Japan 2007; 34: 32-37.

[11] Tanaka H. The Construction of Japanese EHR: New Version of Health Informatics. The Volume of Health Information Systems. Shinoharashinsha, Tokyo, Japan 2009.

Index

A

B

C

D

Shunji Wakamiya, Kazunobu Yamauchi and Hiroyuki Yoshihara (Eds)

E

F

H

S

T

U

W

X

Made in United States
Orlando, FL
04 November 2026

90201089R00105